HUNTERS
WEE STORIES FROM THE CRESCENT

HUNTER CRESCENT

DEDICATION

Dedicated to my family, friends, and the many local characters of Hunters, who collectively made the sixteen years of my life on the estate happy, sad, and everything in-between.

Hunters

Wee Stories from the Crescent

A Reminiscence of Perth's
Hunter Crescent

Anthony Camilleri

TIPPERMUIR
· BOOKS LIMITED ·

Hunters: Wee Stories from the Crescent.
A Reminiscence of Perth's Hunter Crescent
Copyright © Anthony Camilleri 2017.
All rights reserved.
The right of Anthony Camilleri to be identified as the author of
the Work has been asserted by him in accordance with the
Copyright, Designs and Patents Act 1988.
This printed edition published and copyright 2017 by
Tippermuir Books Ltd, Perth, Scotland.
mail@tippermuirbooks.co.uk
www.tippermuirbooks.co.uk

ISBN: 978-0-9954623-6-6 (paperback)
A CIP catalogue record for this book is available from the British Library.

Editorial and project management: Dr Paul S. Philippou.
Editorial support: Ajay Close and Jean Hands.

Cover design Matthew Mackie.
Text styling, layout and cover artwork:
Bernard Chandler [graffik], Glastonbury, England. www.graffik.co.uk
Text set in 11/14pt Bodoni Std Book.

Printed and bound by CPI Group (UK) Ltd, Croydon CR0 4YY.

Contents

Acknowledgements

IN WRITING THIS BOOK it became apparent to me how fondly Hunter Crescent is remembered by many of the people who lived there – from the decades of its heyday, through to the years of its notoriety, neglect, and decline, and finally to its regeneration and rebirth. They recalled how Hunter Crescent became a notorious housing scheme and as the decades rolled on how it seemed the council had given up on it. And how as the 1970s began, realising there were major social and environmental issues the council tried to solve the estate's ills with a sticking-plaster solution: whitewashing the exterior of the buildings and ripping out the gardens – only for this to cause the opposite effect by sending the scheme into the worst period of its history from which it did not begin to recover until the mid to late 1980s – and only then because of a determined group of tenants and supportive organisations.

This book is not *The History of Hunter Crescent*. It is simply my hazy memories of my time there. Any inaccuracies are down to me.

I would also like to thank everyone who helped me. Firstly, the staff of the Perth & Kinross Council Archive and the AK Bell Library (CPK), especially those who work in the archive and local studies sections – they were so generous with their time and had endless amount of patience as I think I asked to see a copy of every old *Perthshire Advertiser* ever published, looking for scraps of information on the Holy Land I know as Hunter Crescent. These parts of the library are a gold mine for local information and I highly recommend them for anyone interested in local history or wishing to research their family tree.

Next, I would also like to thank my friend Brian Little who spent endless hours looking for photographs of the Feus Hoose, the Hunters' chippy, and other photographs that I could use. I also have to mention and thank social media especially the Facebook sites, Happy Hunters Hooligans and Auld Perth Bairns, invaluable resources and contacts. I also have to mention and thank Iain Howie at the *Perthshire Advertiser* for allowing me to use photographs from back issues of the newspaper. I wish to say a big thank you to all the individuals who trusted me with their cherished photographs – it really did mean a lot:

Samantha Allan, Kate Cameron, John Carter, Paula Christie, Davidson, Stella Frampton, Debra Garton, Helen Gillies, James Herd, Dave Hoolachan, Susan Hoolachan, Roxanne Fraser, Irene Graham, John Lloyd, Lynda Malia, Duane McPhee, Fiona McWilliam, Arlene Reaney, Sandy Sampson, Mags Simpson, Harry Smith, Aileen Wallace, and Paula Williamson.

I would also like to thank for her help Sandy Halliday whose late husband worked with Gaia Architects and was an instrumental figure in the Fairfield Village Project.

Thanks too go to Paul Philippou of Tippermuir Books for his support, belief in this project, and for helping to get it off the ground after five years of pitching to other publishers. Paul took a chance with it, which I will be eternally grateful for.

Lastly, thank you to you the reader for buying the book. I hope you enjoy the stories and memories of my childhood in Hunters and hope it may trigger happy memories of your own – whether you lived in Hunter Crescent or not.

Anthony Camilleri

FOREWORD

I GREW UP IN LETHAM on a hillside overlooking the northern
perimeters of Perth. It was the last road on a sprawling housing
scheme, the only road that looked out northwards to the Grampian
Hills and to a highland land I rarely visited. Shakespeare had written
about the bleak conspiratorial forests beyond and predicted a dark
fate for Macbeth *'when Birnam Wood marches to Dunsinane'*. The
area had even taken the names as roadways, I lived only a few
hundred yards from Birnam Crescent and trudged along Dunsinane
Drive on my way to school. There were often witches at the bus stops
at the Strathtay Road terminus where the bus route that that took us
into town began.

When you looked down into the valley below the night stretched
out to Muirton where I first fell in love with the local football club
St Johnstone FC. There was something magical about midweek games,
when the floodlights flickered to life they seemed to match up
with the lights form the railway marshalling yards as they lit up the
rail-tracks north of the town.

To reach the ground by foot, you had to reach the end of the red
brick walls of Dorran's factory. The local gang the Pack had spray
painted the walls, claiming a Dundee gang called the Mental Shimmy
and accusing its leader Felix Dowdalls of being a self-abuser. Then
you had had to navigate a long asphalt path that snaked alongside the
marshalling yards up to a footbridge that took you over to Muirton
Park, the place where Hall and Connolly played. To the right-side of
the path was Hunters, a land that was both chilling and sad. It was
the most socially deprived area of Perth and for a young teenager a
place alive with anxieties and psychopathic characters. I went to
school with boys from Hunters and they always had stories that made
it sound like Harlem or the South Bronx, a ghetto of sorts.

My Uncle Billy who was a fireman told a story that for me remains the best story I've ever heard about Hunters and its unique resilience. In the 1980s, housewives and single mothers had come to realise that they would be re-housed in Letham, and get a better council house if their own home was deemed uninhabitable. Some had taken it into their own hands and set fire to their own homes rushing them and their children to the top of the housing list. One day the alarms went off in the fire station near Feus Road and my uncle held the emergency response team to the site of the fire. When they got there a woman and her two children were sitting on top of all their worldly objects: the carpet had been rolled up neatly, the kitchen utensils were boxed away and the family's television set and stereo unit were neatly stacked together. When the fire engine arrived urgently unravelling hose-pipes and fire blankets the woman said *'It was a close thing. We just got oot in time'*. She was leaving Hunters but never its memories.

Stuart Cosgrove
Stuart Cosgrove is a writer and broadcaster

Hunter Crescent and Fairfield
Housing Co-operative[1]

THE FAIRFIELD VILLAGE PROJECT forms part of a major regeneration project that has involved almost 350 homes and cost more than £20 million. The original housing scheme, Hunter Crescent, designed as Neo-Georgian tenements underwent construction in 1934-6 (along with similar and associated developments by the Crieff Road). The building of Hunter Crescent marked the final stage of Perth's inter-war residential house-building initiative that had taken in the Craigie, Darnhall, Dunkeld Road, Friarton, Hillyland, Riggs Road, and Scott Street areas of the city.

Hunter Crescent thrived as a community for several decades. A key turning point in the social durability of the area was the decision by the local authority in the 1970s to replace the estate's gardens with bleak concrete landscaping.

Social deprivation, rising crime levels, neglect, loss of housing stock, reduced occupancy, environmental decline, failure to update the estate's poor heating/insulation, and lack of maintenance over several decades severely affected the Hunter Crescent community. In 1981 Hunter Crescent was described as *'the most deprived area in Scotland'*. By 1986 unemployment on the estate reached 80 per cent – educational achievement, health, life expectancy, and drug abuse all stood at the wrong end of the spectrum. With a mass of social problems and hundreds of properties unviable the occupancy level of the estate bottomed out.

The regeneration of Hunter Crescent began in the later 1980s and today Fairfield Village Project is a model of sustainability and

---

[1] Source: Paul S. Philippou and Roben Antoniewicz, *Perth: Street by Street* (Tippermuir, 2012).

community action that has led to the area's cultural, physical, and socio-economic regeneration, and a Scottish National Heritage Award (1995). The catalyst for this renewal was the residents themselves who set up Hunter Village (later Fairfield) Housing Co-operative in July 1986.

Each stage of the Fairfield Village Project employed cutting-edge techniques of energy-efficiency and sustainability both in design and realisation. The project unfolded in eight phases and included refurbishment of the existing tenements, the building of several new Sunscoop houses, and the building of Tollhouse Gardens. A key architectural partner in the project was the firm Gaia Architects.

The Fairfield development comprises Angus Court, Douglas Court, Leslie Court, Malcolm Court, McCallum Court, McDonald Court, McKenzie Court, McLeod Court, and Menzies Court. As part of the area's regeneration, the name Fairfield (a nod to the Fair City of Perth) replaced the stigmatised Hunter Crescent.

Of note is Angus Court whose two/three-storey apartment blocks and housing units underwent refurbishment in 1998-9 as phase six of the Fairfield Village Project (Gaia Architects & Locate Architects). In 2008 a group of seven newly built family homes employing very modern architectural design opened at Angus Court. This development received a Perth Civic Trust certificate of high commendation.

In 1997 another Perth Civic Trust award went to Leslie Court (Robin Baker – Gaia Architects) – a commendation for the design of seventeen low-energy apartments.

Morris Court forms part of the Barratt Homes Axiom development and includes four-storey apartment blocks. A section of Morris Court (fifteen one/two-bedroom properties) was acquired in 2009 by Fairfield Housing Co-operative as '*its first off-the-shelf development*'.

The final stage of the Fairfield regeneration project is Tollhouse Gardens. A major aim of the construction of Tollhouse Gardens' fourteen one/two-bedroom apartments was the creation of a low-allergen environment by careful selection of building materials. In 2005 Tollhouse Gardens received a Perth Civic Trust Gold award.

There is a memorial plaque on the front of the Tollhouse Gardens development dated 3 October 2003.

'Ralph Wilson was one of the founder members of Fairfield Housing Co-operative whose perseverance and hard work have transformed Fairfield. This development is dedicated to his memory.'

CHAPTER ONE

A Housing Scheme 'Far, Far, Away'

HUNTER CRESCENT, a sprawling housing scheme approximately a mile north of Perth city centre that included Hunter Crescent, Hunter Terrace, Ruthven Avenue, Ruthven Place, and Tulloch Road, came to be because of a government Act passed in the early twentieth century that called for the removal of slum areas and their replacement with modern housing. At the time Perth's city centre slum housing, such as those in Thimblerow and Castle Gable, comprised overpopulated tenement properties in narrow streets. These were to be demolished. Most of the families living in these slum areas were designated to be rehoused in a modern housing scheme of some 200 houses constructed in the Crieff Road area of the city of Perth.

Praise for this initiative must go primarily to the Perth labour and trade union movements that had been advocating and campaigning for housing reform from the 1890s onwards but also to Sir Thomas Hunter (Provost of Perth, 1932-5, and Scottish Unionist MP for Perth, 1935-45) who was proactive in his response to demands for improvements to the lives of local people living in substandard accommodation.

It was decided by the local authority that the new housing scheme, which was designed by Thomas McLaren (Burgh Surveyor) and John Alexander William Grant (Advising Architect) and which took approximately three years to build, would be called Hunter Crescent. Another name mooted at the time was Jubilee Crescent.

For its first thirty-five years Hunter Crescent was a model of how a housing scheme should be. Little did anyone know during that period that by the mid-1970s things would have gone horribly wrong and it would be a group of tenants who would take the lead in putting 'Hunters', as the estate became known, back on an even keel.

Some people blame Hunters' woes on an influx of Travellers rehoused in Hunter Crescent after the local authority started to clear the campsites around the River Almond. Nothing could be further from the truth. Like all communities there were good and bad. The truth is the council lost interest in maintaining, repairing, and updating Hunter Crescent and its housing stock started to fall into disrepair – a process that continued at a rapid pace.

It would be fair to say that the glory days of Hunter Crescent were the 1950s and the 1960s. Talking to some of the older residents they will tell you of that time:

'Ye could leave your door open and naebody would steal a thing'.

Of course, this was probably because there was nothing to steal.

Another line often used when former Hunter Crescent residents reminisce about the immediate postwar decades signifies the estate's community spirit:

'If you needed a wee drop sugar your next-door neighbour would help you out'.

By the 1970s those days were sadly gone, although as rough as it eventually got, and there were many family feuds, Hunter Crescent was still a tight-knit community of people who for the most part would help each other out.

Only a generation of people can appreciate the transformation of Hunter Crescent to Fairfield Village, especially those who grew up in its darkest periods, the 1970s and 1980s. Back then it was a haven for drug addicts, glue sniffers, high unemployment, and crime (two per cent of all crime in Tayside took place in Hunter Crescent in 1985). The estate was considered to be one of the most deprived areas in the whole of Scotland, and indeed in Europe.

At one time there were almost 2,000 people living on the estate but by the mid-1980s occupancy was at an all-time low of just over 500; and a high proportion of properties on the estate were boarded up with wooden panels or corrugated iron sheeting. All in all it could be an intimidating place during daylight hours but at night it was a no-go area for outsiders and even the locals were wary of going out after dark. One national newspaper reported that when answering a call the local constabulary would send two police cars: one to handle the complaint, the other to guard the cars so they couldn't be stolen.

After years of tenant power the estate was rejuvenated and fully occupied. All the properties were updated with new fixtures and fittings, freshly decorated, double glazed, and secured with security doors … a far cry from the living conditions of earlier. Now there are beautifully maintained parks, no more broken slabs or loose cobbles, just tidy parking bays.

The firm of Gaia Architects has to be given great credit for the quality of the regeneration, turning a housing estate with hundreds of empty homes into one in very high demand. It was Howard Liddell of Gaia who convinced the local authority not to demolish the estate and instead to convert its structurally-sound buildings into high-end homes. The estate went on to win a World Habitat Commendation in 2003.

My mum and dad (Rachel and Fred) moved into 11D Hunter Crescent in April 1967. After a period renting a one-bedroom flat in Shore Road for £1.10s, they were delighted to move up in the world to what was then a desirable part of Perth to live … even if the rent was a steep £2 per week. The following year I was delivered by the stork. It was 1968 and it was still safe for storks to fly over Hunters' airspace. Three years later my brother John was brought home by my mum in an ambulance – storks refused to land by the start of the 1970s.

We Camilleris lived in Hunter Crescent from 1967 until 1984. I recall how in April of 1984 my mum gave us the news that we were getting our Aunty Jenny's house in Brahan Terrace in the Letham area of Perth. We got permission for the transfer from the council after my Aunty Jenny had told them she would leave all the white goods if her niece got the property. I am sad to say I cannot remember my last day in Hunter Crescent. By then most of my friends had moved on but it was an end to an era, a big part of my early life that even today I look back on with fond happy memories.

11D Hunter Crescent had all mod cons including hot and cold running water and an inside toilet. We had a fairly big living room, which I always remember being wallpapered in woodchip and painted purple, brown, or a groovy green – furnished with a matching cream leatherette suite to match. It was the height of the 1970s and no one could afford an interior designer. We didn't have a fancy hi-fi stacking sound system. We had a mahogany radiogram that you opened at the top to find a record player. Once you placed the record on the deck you would then lower the arm onto it. You would have to place a couple of two pence coins on it to stop it from jumping. Our record collection lacked any real depth: a couple of Elvis albums, Dean Martin's *Greatest Hits*, and a load of those 1970s *Top of the Pops* albums where some no-mark singer would do a cover version of a big hit by a superstar or the band of the day. This was the kind of music you used to hear in the supermarket before they went all trendy and started their own radio stations.

Our television was a black and white set. It was powered by a tube that had the life of a midgie in January. In the middle of *Coronation Street,* when Ken Barlow was about to stick the heed into Mike Baldwin, the screen would go black but for a little white spot in the middle of the screen. It became the norm that we knew the routine. Dad would go out, come back about an hour later with a television, which he had bought from a supplier in Ruthven Avenue (most likely to have been Eric the Pole who had everything from screwdrivers to televisions for sale). The newly-purchased television was usually the size of and shape of a depth charge and possessed two space-age buttons on the top. One was for volume and the other for the multitude of channels to choose from ... all three of them – BBC1, BBC2 and ITV!

Some families had something called the Relay that gave you access to STV, which in turn meant you got *Glen Michael's Cartoon Cavalcade,* a weekly cartoon show on a Sunday afternoon. It was a great event if one of your pals invited you back to their house to watch it. A few families had slot televisions with a meter attached. I think you got about four hours of viewing for 50p. The television man from Radio Rentals, DER or Rediffusion would come once a month and empty the box.

It never ceases to amaze me how there was always something to watch on these three-channel black and white televisions (we didn't get a colour television until 1978 – for the World Cup in Argentina). Now I have hundreds of channels and can find nothing worth watching. In the winter, if there was a good film on, my mum would say '*Put the big light out'*, which was the main room light, and *'Put the wee light on'*, which was a table lamp. With the coal fire roaring it was a cosy night in.

The centrepiece of the living room was the big black coal fire with mantelpiece that could only be described as the same one *The Broons* have. It was later replaced by a bland cream-tiled fireplace that had as much character as one of our local councillors. You can say what you like about modern central heating systems but you cannot beat a roaring coal fire. I remember skewering bread through with a poker to make toast and feeling like the Big Man watching the bread turn golden brown. I also used to have great fun throwing plastic soldiers and Airfix models into the fire until my mum would catch me and start shouting: *'Git away fae there you'll put the bloody lum up!'*.

My defence that they had fallen off the mantelpiece always fell on deaf ears.

Years later as a teenager I would be allowed to get the fire started, which took real skill. Sheets of yesterday's newspaper would be twisted up and used as a base – some sticks would be built up and if you were lucky a fire-lighter (or a wee bit of lard) was added to help light the fire. You would then start to add the coal. Sometimes to help it along you would cover the front of the fireplace with a large sheet of newspaper to increase the draught and to help the fire on but nine times out of ten the paper would catch fire and head up the chimney like a magic lantern. Eventually I went high tech and balanced the shovel on the grate, which worked better than newspaper.

Our hallway was long and narrow with what would seem alien now, a coal cellar on the right-hand side. The kitchen was slightly wider than a galley kitchen with a gas cooker and a twin tub washing machine that would jump about the kitchen like a bucking bronco. My job was to sit next to it with my foot on the bottom to stop it galloping down the hall as it went through its final spin cycle. We also had a washing board that my mum would use to remove tidemarks from white school shirts. I can also remember a clothes ringer and on numerous occasions getting my finger or hair caught in it. Every house in Hunter Crescent had a pulley, which had clothes hanging from it 24/7. Only problem with that was your clothes would smell of chips and egg, liver and onions, or whatever delights you had for tea the night before.

I remember when I was very young we had a larder that had an air vent to keep foodstuff cool. I even remember the excitement of getting our first fridge – one that had a small freezer drawer in it! In the corner of the kitchen, sitting on an old chair, we had an old 1950s radio – a beast of a thing that could pick up radio stations from far off places a boy from Hunters had never heard of – Lisbon, Barcelona, Moscow, and Dundee!

I have many a happy memory of me and my best pal Willie Burns sitting in the winter months in the kitchen, with the gas oven on for heat and the windows covered in condensation, listening to the football on that radio – Bob Crampsey usually telling us who St Johnstone were getting beat by. Unlike the modern kitchens of today the water tank and pipes were not hidden behind fancy fittings and in the winter, during the harsh cold weather, it was not uncommon to lag the water tank with an old jacket and go along the pipes with a lit candle to stop them freezing.

The bathroom was tiny with 1970s black plastic fittings. No one in Hunters was posh enough to have avocado. The council had at the time said:

'You can have it in any colour as long as it is black'.

The toilet was from a bygone age with the cistern above the throne, and to this day I still tell children to *'pull the chain'* rather than flush when they have used the toilet.

The tiles behind the sink and bath were white. I decorated them with those rub on tattoos you used to get with chewing gum. One tile could have a rocket, the next a dragon, then a tennis ball. It didn't catch on but they stayed on those tiles till the day we left in 1984.

The bedrooms were only slightly warmer than a Siberian morgue and notoriously cold, with Jack Frost leaving his trademark inside and outside the single-pane windows. To keep warm we had bed sheets, candlewick bedding, crochet bedding made of odd balls of wool, and fancy quilts with sleeves or as I like to call them Old Jackets. To complement them we would have an empty TC lemonade bottle filled with hot water then covered with an old football sock to add to the warmth of your bed. The closest thing to central heating was placing a paraffin heater into the middle of the bedroom but this could be costly as you would have to open the window to let the fumes out. If we ran out of paraffin I would sometimes be sent to Birrell's Garage on the Crieff Road with a plastic bottle, as they had a self-service Esso Blue paraffin pump – I think it cost about 30p to fill a bottle.

One big plus point was the view from my bedroom window. I could see Simpson Park, the home of Jeanfield Swifts, and must have watched hundreds of games from that bedroom window.

Single-pane sash and case windows were no good for keeping heat in, were poor security, and not much of a deterrent for keeping out the local house-breakers. You would maybe be surprised to hear no one had close-circuit television or burglar alarms. Most windows would be nailed so they could only open about four inches. It wasn't uncommon for neighbours on the second and third floors to pour old chip fat on the drain pipes to stop the more agile house-breakers from helping themselves. We had the misfortune of one of the said gentleman breaking into our house and robbing the meter. The case went to court but because it was all on hearsay and because Hunters operated its own version of *Omertà*, the Mafia code of silence (known locally as '*keep yer puss shut*'), no one would testify. The next day, while at Scott's paper shop, the alleged thief offered me 50p to which my granny told him to stuff it somewhere which wasn't his wallet.

Our house, like everyone else's, had an electric meter and like many people my dad would try all sorts of dodges to get cheap or free electricity. He would use old washers and foreign coins. When it came time to empty the meter the Lecky Man would pile up the ten pences into equal amounts and put the washers, foreign coins, and old currency in another. My dad would then say in an accusing manner in broken English whilst pointing at me:

'*It's him, I keepa telling hima no to do it but he a no listen*'.

Right enough, at the age of seven it was at the top of my list how to get economical energy prices. It was quite an occasion when the Lecky Man came. He would write something in a dog-eared filthy note book and put the money in an equally grubby small satchel he would have over his shoulder. Occasionally you would get a small rebate of sorts. Not sure how accurate the whole thing was to be honest.

Another dodge was to cut a thin piece of lino to stop the meter reader from going around – a pin or magnet could also be used.

The closes in Hunters in the main were kept clean by neighbours who would take a turn at sweeping and mopping once a week – the fumes from bleach or disinfectant would catch the back of your throat. The closes had glass blocks to let in light and this is where some of the biggest spiders and moths you have ever seen would congregate.

It was the same with the gardens. They were well maintained, as were the drying greens at the back of the houses. Neighbours even had an allocated day for using the washing lines. You would get the odd garden that looked like the Sahara grasslands with grass growing up to four feet and bushes towering over the fence. You were always wary of a herd of zebra charging out or being chased by a lion or a wild strain of mongrel.

This was an era when you knew your neighbours and I can still remember everyone in our block of six. Underneath us we had Willie Ferguson, his wife Helen, and her son Steven. Upstairs we had the Browns (the Broons), May and her two daughters, Angie and Marlynn (my brother and I were often babysat by the sisters as my mum and dad would be working when we finished school, which was great as they had a colour television and a miniature snooker table ... two things we didn't have). The Costellos, Katie, her son Mark, and daughter Kelly, lived next door to the Browns. Mark was part of our group and even when towards the end of his teens he spent more time at his granny's on the Dunkeld Road, he didn't forget his allegiance to the Hunters flag. Our next-door neighbours were Mr and Mrs Heath, the loveliest people you could ever meet. Mr Heath was a doorman at the local cinema and once held me upside down by my ankles when I was choking on a toffee apple. After a couple of slaps on the back, all was good – I'd like to add I was about two years old and was the svelte-like creature that I no longer am. Mrs Heath was a lovely lady who always wore a pinnie and I am presuming she cooked a lot as the smells that used to waft out of their house would have you salivating: mince and tatties, home made scones, and soup. Oh, and they were posh – they had a cuckoo clock.

Finally at 11A Hunter Crescent, we had the Conterios, Joe, Carol, and their son Karl. My wee brother used to drive Karl demented threatening to batter him and chasing him when he was minding his own business. His mum, Carol, was always smiling and I think a bit of a free spirit, as I remember her a few times making soup with nettles, grass, and dandelions collected from their overgrown back garden. Another posh neighbour was my pal Cathrine Sinclair who stayed at 9 Hunter Crescent. Her dad had built her a sandpit and sometimes she let me play in it if she got to wash my hair with pretend shampoo made of sand.

Then in the mid-1970s, some chinless wonder, some urban planner who at some stage in his or her life spent time behind the iron curtain, decided it was time to upgrade Hunters into something that resembled a Soviet housing scheme. The buildings were to be whitewashed and the gardens ripped out (without consultation) and replaced by soulless cobbles and concrete slabs. The area became so blighted that by the mid-1980s it was commonly agreed by local councillors that the only option was to put *'a bomb under it'*.

CHAPTER TWO

The Good the Bad and the Berrygrubbers

ALL THOSE who grew up in my generation in Hunter Crescent would more than likely have spent their summers at the Berries, usually at Easter Essendy near Blairgowrie. Not many, in fact no one I knew, went to Florida for the school summer holidays. Instead we got nice healthy tans grubbing in the fields of Perthshire – not by lying on a beach in Miami.

Gooseberries (also known as goosegogs) were an awful fruit to pick as the bushes were covered in sharp thorns that would leave you covered in scratches and looking like an extra from a Bruce Lee movie. The strawberries (the strawbs) were a back-breaking task. I hated them. I used to pick them on my knees. By the end of the day, the knees of my trousers were covered in the squashed strawberries I had knelt on. Blackcurrant was another berry variety we would pick. Blackcurrants were a waste of time and I am sure they were full of air, as no matter how much you crammed into your pail you would still get the same paltry amount of money. The berry of choice for all the Hunters grubbers was the raspberry, that's where the real money could be made and more importantly the fun was endless.

Before you got near a berry field, you had to be interrogated by one of the godmothers of the berry business. The three I remember are: Mrs Smith, a tiny wee woman who walked around the field with a stick, a smile, and a fag in her mouth. She was a lovely woman who was always laughing; Mrs MacDonald who knew all her pickers by name; and then there was Mrs Carnegie who always had an impressive array of tomato plants in her living room window.

The interview was short and sharp, usually consisting of three questions:

'*Where do you live?*',
'*Who's yer mum?*',

and

'Have you been to the Berries before?'.

If you were successful, you were told to be at a certain place in the Crescent and at what time the next morning.

The day would usually start with getting on the berry bus in the middle of Hunters. The bus may have been built in the late 1960s to drive round a nice suburb of a market town in England and designed to seat 38 passengers and 16 standing but it had fallen on hard times. Safety rules didn't apply to a berry bus being used for passengers from a notorious housing scheme in Scotland. All shapes and sizes of kids and adults would be squashed onto the bus. Kids sat on their parents' knees, people crammed in the space usually reserved for suitcases, and the aisles were packed so tight with bodies you could smell what they had for breakfast, which could be anything from a Carlsberg Special to black coffee and a fag. All dressed like tramps we would jump aboard the bus that at best was borderline roadworthy – broken seats, smashed windows, and even large holes on the floor were the norm.

I was lucky enough to be driven to the berries by Eck Morison. Eck was always the odd one out. He was usually dressed in an old suit, shirt and tie, and sporting slick hair. An unforgettable smell only found on a berry bus of fag smoke, sweat, pish, and diesel, usually confirmed you were in first class. You should have seen and smelled the cheap seats. The bus would stop and pick other grubbers up on the way. I can vaguely remember two or three getting on at North Muirton, a world away from where we lived – and I often wondered whether they were on the bus as a dare or a bet.

As you approached the berry field, the real grubbers, the berry pickers, would peer out of the filthy or cracked windows and with the wise eyes of experienced pickers would declare to everyone that the berries were *'hingin'*. They didn't see the fruit as berries, they saw them as cold hard cash and it was there for the taking. I was a terrible picker usually going home with no more than £5 for about eight hours work if I was lucky. The money was usually kept in a sock with a knot tied tight.

When we arrived everyone jumped off the bus like troops going into battle. Depending on what the berries were being used for would determine if you were given a basket or a bucket – baskets would be for jam and buckets for berries for the dyeing industry.

Buckets could also be called luggies, which is a Scottish word meaning small wooden pails or dishes with a handle. At the same time as running to get either you would be tying a piece of orange string around your waist – a grumpy farm worker playing the part of a German POW camp guard pointing you to your dreel with a stick and bawling:

'Nae fucking about fae you two!',

'Start at the top of the dreel!',

or

'I'll be checking your picking clean!'.

Every berry was priceless to the farmer.

Surprisingly there was no catering supplied by the farmer, so you had to bring your own. Lunch was usually pieces with spreading cheese, spam, chopped pork, or my favourite Shippam's fish and meat pastes. (I can also recall some grubbers having beetroot sandwiches.) All of this could be washed down with a flask of stewed tea, cheap coffee, or a selection of cold drinks including TC orangeade, cola, apple, and cream soda, to name a few. I have seen a few poor buggers who had a sandwich that consisted of Echo margarine (one step up from spreadable candle wax) and squashed raspberries, and a flask of stewed tea to wash it down. Sometimes your mum would give you diluting juice that was only slightly stronger than water and tasted like cat pish … and was usually warm by lunchtime. You would never share your juice in fear of a berry-picking comrade leaving floaters in your bottle, no matter how thirsty they were.

Most of the berry picking we did was in Blairgowrie. There were also fields out in the Gask area near the Dundee Road. The Glaswegian division of berry pickers were based at Easter Essendy and spent the summer there, billeted in concrete huts with metal sheet roofing. We all got on very well as we shared the same sense of humour and could be quite vocal if we thought someone was taking the piss, especially the farmer. I remember us all going on strike for three hours for 2p extra on every pound of berries we picked. Everyone remained at the bottom of their dreels until the farmer buckled and gave us our 2p pay rise. The only down side of this industrial action was we had all eaten our pieces before ten o'clock.

Another group of amazing berry pickers were the Travellers. From the adults to the young children, they were all great grubbers and had a great work ethic. The Travellers I knew would work in teams with their mother as the accountant. Some of them would not stop picking all day, breaking only to have a slurp of lemonade before heading back up the dreel again. Just like the Glaswegians they were great entertainers, especially when it came to singing Sometimes, you could swear that Aretha Franklin or Elvis Presley was in the next dreel.

You were paid by weight. There were some world-class pickers who could make a pile. They were Olympic class, trained to pick a fortune. They could pick three times as much as I could. They would squash their berries down until they had a bucket of raspberry pulp and they would have to tag up with their picking partner to take it to the weights.

All sorts of dodges were used to bulk up the weight of your bucket from putting boulders in with your berries (but if you were caught doing that you were thrown off the field never to come back again and left to do the walk of shame out of Blairgowrie) to peeing in it which I found pointless unless you could pee like a horse. The weights were usually determined on the back of a large trailer manned by a miserable farmer who looked like Scrooge in a flat cap. He would empty the berries into a set of scales and you would then be paid a few coins for three-hours effort, knowing you had to go back and start again.

It was always a bonus to get a dreel next to someone with a transistor radio. At the time Simon Bates was a big star on Radio 1. His show had a daily segment called *Our Tune*, which went with a tear-jerking story about love lost, found again, then lost. It was total cheese but at the time people loved it. What made it were the comments from the berry field as some poor soul's story was being read out:

'*How could the bitch do that?*',

'*He's no worth it hen!*',

and

'*Better withoot her Big Man!*'.

Then a sad song would be played and again the berry field agony aunts would join in yelping like dogs or howling like wolves to the music.

My picking partner of choice was my best pal Willie. He was, as they used to say, a '*wee short arse*'. I would steal all the berries he couldn't reach on the top.

If I went with my mum, she usually picked with Evelyn McCullie, which meant I would get to pick with her daughter Tracy who was a bit of a berry-field hottie. Although a little-known fact is that Erica Williamson was my first berry-field wife ... think I was about twelve – her wedding ring was made of the famous orange string we tied round our waist to hold our pails and baskets.

A Perthshire summer comes with the guarantee of rain. It's a rain that falls like a tsunami from above, and when it rained at the Berries the dreels could flood and small rivers could run down the dreels. We would all head back to the Glaswegian berry pickers' reservation. You could not meet a more welcoming friendly bunch of people than the Glaswegians living in those huts. They would offer you a life-saving cup of tea and a biscuit as you dried off next to the fire. It wasn't uncommon for the guitar to come out and someone would murder a selection of Elvis and Patsy Cline songs. It was all good fun and the humour was top class.

Luckily something that didn't happen to me but did to a lot of friends, was getting your berries stolen. It was like someone ripping your heart out and pishing on it – the reality of hours of work taken from you by a berry thief in no more than a minute. There was a certain amount of trust at the Berries. As you filled plastic baskets with berries you would leave them in your dreel as you went. Now and again some thief would sniper through the bushes and steal them as you were picking away further up, dreaming of what you were going to buy with your money. There was one episode, which I am sure has grown arms and legs over the years. The way I remember it was I thought I was picking away not near anyone – it was a beautiful hot July day – suddenly, about ten feet away from me, an angry call went out:

'*Thieving bastard!*'.

Then like a ninja in rags a body came flying over the bushes landing on their feet followed by a second ninja also in rags almost immediately galloping down the dreel. The pursuer took one of his boots off and threw it towards the runner successfully hitting him on the back of the head and knocking him off his feet. This in turn was followed by a flurry of punches and chops with the thief pleading that it was a misunderstanding and he thought they were his berries … even though his dreel was in another part of the field.

Mrs Smith's son Albert used to go to the Berries. He could do the best animal impersonations you have ever heard, from a rabbit to a snow leopard. One day in the middle of the afternoon the sound of a bull bellowed up and down the berry field. Then the shout from Albert went up:

'*Run there's a bull in the field, run for your life!*' .

The sound of about sixty people running down dreels of berries is spectacular. As we all got the bottom of the dreels, Albert was standing there bellowing like a bull. A few days later, he impersonated the sound of an elephant telling us to run for our lives as a herd of elephants were trampling through the dreels. It didn't have the same shock factor, besides we knew it was a hoax – you don't get elephants in Blairgowrie … if he had said giraffes, we might have believed him.

Apart from semi-poisonous snakes there is nothing at the Berries that can do you any real harm. However, Scotland has some of the most savage insects known to mankind. It's a roll call of pain. In no specific order: fleas, wasps, spiders, horseflies, bluebottles, and ticks – and you would find them all in a berry field. The one I feared the most was the wasp. I must have been stung about ten times over the years at the Berries. The worst one ever was getting stung under the armpit. I remember rolling on the floor in agony. Ann Leaver came out of nowhere, picked the sting out, and then wiped it with a dock leaf. She was like a 1970s female Bear Grylls.

Berry picking was a long day and the call of nature was inevitable. We had no fancy Portaloos back then. Instead, you tended to go downwind of your dreel. A pee wasn't an issue, you just peed where you stood and got straight back to making money. A *Number Two* was more problematic. You would kick a hole with your heel into the ground, do your business, quickly wipe your bum with a dock leaf, newspaper or if you were posh, toilet paper, then you would hastily cover it before a swarm of bluebottles made short work of it.

Berry fights were part and parcel of the day in the field. Between lobbing berries over the dreels or someone sneaking up behind you and rubbing a handful of berries in your face there was always danger. My chosen style of berry assault was to grab a handful of berries, squash them into a pulp, and just throw them into the air covering a large area making a machinegun sound as they hit bushes and victims' skin. It was crude but very effective. You knew you had a direct hit when you heard the calls of anger:

'*Who the fuck threw that?*',

'*Grow up*',

and the curiously confident

'*That just hit my bairn, I'll be seeing you on the bus!*'.

You would usually see your victims on the bus going home covered in berry stains cursing the phantom berry thrower and not realising you were among them.

One sound of the Blairgowrie countryside we all feared was the '*ting-ting-ting*' of the ice cream van entering the berry field. It was the most unnatural sight you could imagine. In between Massey Fergusson, John Deere, and Land Rovers was this small ice cream van playing *Whistle While You Work* as it entered the field. The ice cream man wanted what we had in our tied sock and some of us fell for the charms he had. His timing was always bang on. He would turn up, usually on a rare very hot day, and shout:

'*Aye I've chilled those cans of Coke in the freezer!*'

or

'*Aye an orange Mivvi will quench yer thirst!*'.

I can remember one greedy farmer banning ice cream vans from the berry field and banning berry pickers from leaving the field to buy anything. In fact he would, if he could, have banned everyone from his berry field. The next day he opened his own tuck shop charging prices that would make the local corner shop blush! I was always under strict instructions from my mum not to waste my money at the van. It would break my heart seeing others buying Fabs, Mivvis, 99s, or Merlins. Meanwhile, I would be taking my last gulp of warm limeade.

The day would end with a final call:

'Berry up!'.

That was the signal for everyone to weigh-in and head for the bus. This is when the tall tales would begin:

'No as much as yesterday – made about £19 I think'

– when most other grubbers would be taking home between maybe £5 and £7.

They must have been on a bonus, half-man half-spider, or stealing my berries.

The Williamsons were all great pickers, especially Shuggie Williamson. He could fill two luggies to my one.

Once the bus crammed full of tired pickers left the farm the singing would begin. We were like a bunch of Deep South cotton pickers singing at the top of our voices:

'The front of the bus is in the huff',

'Jenny and John up a tree k-i-s-s-i-n-g',

and

'Big ship that's leaving Bombay' were a few of the songs that you would hear on a regular occurrence.

Some of the songs would make a drill-sergeant blush.

Fashion icons like Gaynor McLean, Arlene Reaney, and Erica Frampton would bore you on the bus about how they were going to Virgo's Fashion Boutique to buy Rah-rah skirts, Dolly Shoes, or pink leg warmers (all 1980s fashion disasters).

It was a hard day's graft. You would get home, have a bath, sit down, and have your tea, sometimes nodding off ten minutes later but I loved it and couldn't wait to get back out there the next day. The camaraderie was top class. Most of us young grubbers were picking to help put money towards school clothing and treats for ourselves. I remember saving up for a pair of football boots – Puma Kings. I think they cost about £25 – a berry pickers ransom back in the early 1980s.

They were the best boots I ever had. It was like playing football in your slippers, they were so comfy. Alas, I didn't have them long, probably about six months. I had been playing football on a muddy pitch, so upon reaching home, I cleaned them and put them outside our front door to dry. By the next day some lousy thief had stolen them.

It would be months before I found the culprit. I was up the grass field known as the *Dump* watching a game when I spied a man of about 5' 2" wearing them. Now I had size 11 feet back then and with his short frame he looked like Bozo the Clown from Billy Smart's Circus. He must have had to stuff about three copies of the *Perthshire Advertiser* in both feet.

Towards the end of the summer the shows (funfair) would be in Perth and as a treat my mum, me, and my brother would head down to the South Inch. This was big deal. The butterflies would start as you headed down Scott Street and heard the music playing. Then as you went round the corner into Marshall Place and you could see all the fancy lights, it was *'SHOWTIME!'*. It was like Las Vegas for a kid from Hunters. Mum would sit and play bingo on the stall that had been coming for years with the same guy, with a voice like a wasp in a jar, belting out the numbers:

'On the yellow line fifty-eight ... on the yellow line fifty-eight'.

A shriek of *'HOUSE'* would go up, the numbers would be checked, and anything from a fondue set to a lava lamp could be won. By this time John and I were feeling queasy with the hot dogs and candy floss we had gorged on.

On another occasion the wrestling was on at the City Hall so I persuaded my dad to take me. The place was packed and a lot of the berry grubbers from Hunters were there. Andy Robins was fighting some English guy called Rollerball Rocco. Things weren't quite going his way so he started winding up the crowd calling us Scottish so-and-sos. Then a *gentleman* from Hunters threw a chair into the ring, then someone else threw a chair, and it just snowballed from there. The ring was covered with chairs but what I remember about it was John Kenny, a Hunters resident, who was a corner man for one of the wrestlers, decided to climb into the ring and tell a packed City Hall to calm down. When that didn't work he took the microphone and started singing *Flower of Scotland*. Everyone in the hall joined in, before the local police asked the crowd to leave the building – great entertainment.

We would finish up in early August and would not see the countryside again until October and the Tattie Holidays – a traditional school holiday invented to allow schoolchildren to help bring in the potato harvest. It was never quite the same as the Berries. The money was better but it was hard graft and it was all business. Adults would pick a bit, kids would get a half-bit. How many yards that is I don't know.

It was always cold and damp. There was no romance of the berries with summer sun and music. It was cold and you tended to be hit by icy autumnal winds. At lunchtime you would turn a wooden crate on its side for shelter just to try and keep out of the cold. Sometimes picking would be put back an hour because the ground was still frozen and too hard for the plough to harvest the potatoes. You would tend to wear two shirts, a jersey, an old jacket, and a hat as well as an old pair of jammie bottoms under your jeans. It was backbreaking work picking tatties.

Although there were no insects, there were worms the size of small snakes and there was always the fear of putting your hand through a rotten tattie. You would try to pick all the shaws from your bit before the tractor came along to plough the tatties to make it easier for you. You couldn't slow down at this caper. It was relentless unless the tractor or plough broke down. Some of the battle-hardy pickers would strategically place stones the size of gravestones in the dreels to damage the machinery as there was an unwritten law that if you worked to lunchtime you would get a full day's pay. You would get a glimmer of hope when further up the field a plume of smoke and the sound of twisted metal could be heard. At that stage a team of farmers would appear that would put a crew of Formula One mechanics to shame getting it started again.

At the end of the day you would go back to the farmer's van and be handed a brown envelope with your pay in it and you would have to sign a ledger. Young ones didn't have to sign it but it was like a *Who's Who* for autograph collectors. You have no idea how many famous people were in the back of that transit van: Lord Lucan, Spiderman, Maggie Thatcher to name a few. I think we even had Red Rum at one stage. How he managed to pick tatties with his hooves I will never know – and of course this had nothing to do with the Brew being after them.

Incidentally the Transit van was a wet dream for Messrs Health & Safety. They would cram the pickers into the back of this rusty van where there was no seating and you would have to sit on spare tyres, tool kits, petrol cans, and other people's knees. The two seats next to the driver were kept for the top pickers.

CHAPTER THREE

999

ONLY ONCE was my collar felt by the long arm of the law ... *'honest your honour'*. It was during a heated game of kick the can. I had found a great hiding space at the side of Scott's paper shop where there was a mound of tarmac that had been dumped there years earlier. Just as I lay like a sniper behind it I caught the image of what looked like a nine-foot policeman. He pointed at me and shouted:

'GET YER ARSE OVER HERE NOW!'.

I stood up and walked towards him like a man condemned. As soon as I got to him, he started shouting at me:

'You were trying to break into the shop, somebody was watching you, dinnae deny it'.

He took out his wee black book and boomed:

'NAME?'.

When I said Anthony Camilleri, he looked at me as if was speaking Chinese, put his note book away, and said:

'Git yer arse up the road, if I see you round here again you're getting lifted'.

As I turned my back he kicked me in the backside with his size twelve boot. It lifted me off my feet like somebody out of a Charlie Chaplin movie. I managed to limp back to the close door of where I lived at 11D Hunter Crescent – sitting there, my face covered in tears and snotters.

There are probably hundreds of police stories that people reading this book could fill another dozen more books with. I believe the police back then tarred us all with the same brush:

'We were not to be trusted',

and

'We were in the most part thieves and liars'.

To be fair to the police they probably did deal with all the above in

Hunter Crescent but they were only a small minority of Hunters folk.

If they stopped you while you were walking through another housing scheme and you said you were from Hunters, they would ask what you were doing, and if they didn't believe you, they would give you five minutes to leave.

To be honest I didn't see the police that much in Hunters. I remember on one occasion, however, a Traveller started playing his guitar about two in the morning singing his favourite Johnny Cash numbers. After three or four songs a police panda car appeared. Two policemen got out of the tiny car.

I was very young and just a trainee curtain-twitcher. I had to move to the other side of my bedroom window and slightly open the window to see and hear what was happening. As the policemen approached Hunters' very own Johnny Cash they grabbed his guitar. In the ensuing scuffle one of the policeman *accidentally* dropped the guitar and *accidentally* put his foot through the back of it. All hell broke loose and like a WWF wrestler the Traveller grabbed the two coppers and somehow manhandled them back into their police panda car. They sped off back over the Crieff Road bridge leaving our very own Johnny Cash wannabe to pick up his broken guitar ... and dreams.

A footnote to the story is the police turned up the next day with more men asking if anyone knew where the guitar man lived but, as I mentioned earlier, the Hunters vow of silence meant no one said anything.

I was never much of a fighter. In fact if anyone hit me when I was a kid I would run home in tears. It was standard practice for Hunters parents to tell you to go back out and hit them back. Usually what happened in my case was my wee brother would go out and knock them out for me.

A fight would usually consist of the combatants bobbing up and down like a couple of kangaroos, then it would all kick off with pulling of hair and a flurry of punches. Sometimes an adult would appear with a *'hey, what's going on there?'* and we would all scarper.

Occasionally you would get some brave soul cutting through

Hunters – usually via the White Bridge. They were the antelope and the Hunters boys were the lions – and if you have ever seen a wildlife documentary you will know how it ended. The poor bugger was probably trying to save himself a fifteen minute round trip, which meant going over the Crieff Road bridge to get home for his tea. People tended to walk that wee bit quicker the minute they turned left into Hunters off the White Bridge but without fail they would be clocked by a *pride* of Hunters feral gangs. Once the victim started running the chase was on. It usually ended with them being tripped up followed by a flurry of punches and kicks. Once they were bored the *pride* would release its prey who would then be seen hobbling past Scott's paper shop and across the road up in to Unity Terrace. The bad lads in Hunters were very territorial ... and proud of the Crescent!

Coal was like black gold in Hunters and there was – thanks to the railway goods yard directly across the rail tracks from the estate – to excuse the pun, a black market in the stuff. Teams of men would go out and like 1920s bootleggers they would go around the doors taking orders. Some families could not have a bath because it was full of coal. Some even used a bedroom to store bags of coal. Occasionally the police would get a tip off and be waiting for those coming back with or delivering Hunters' black gold.

I can remember one time sitting on a climbing frame – we called them monkey bars – watching a small man running while carrying a bag of coal on his back. He looked like a wee turtle running on his back legs with two policemen in hot pursuit. Even with the bag of coal on his back they couldn't quite get to him. We were cheering him on yelling:

'GO ON WEE MAN!' .

Just as he was on the verge of being caught he leapt over a broken corrugated fence and ran up a close with the boys in blue chasing him. After a good ten minutes the police returned to the close door without the *Fastest Coalman in the West,* only to be rudely interrupted by him, minus the bag of coal, sprinting between them – sending them flying. It was like a scene from a Keystone Cops movie.

The police of the 1970s and 80s had a qualification in common sense, something the police of today seem to lack. They were also nine feet tall and built like a brick shithouse. The police of today look about fifteen, have tattoos, and goatee beards. Back then if a problem could be solved without writing out a twelve-page report they were all for it.

We had a neighbour who when coming home drunk late on a Friday would bang up to us shouting:

'Away back tae yer ane country ya black bastards!'.

My dad put up with it for a while then went down and tickled the neighbour's chin with his fist. The next day, the police were at our door. My mum and dad went through the whole story of weeks of abuse. The hulk of a policeman sat down, took his hat off, looked at my dad, and said:

'Fred, I'm no telling you this but the best thing to do is to get him in the back green and rap his puss ... but make sure no one sees you'.

I spoke to a retired policeman while writing this book and he looked back fondly at Hunter Crescent and the camaraderie, saying that on most occasions there was never a grudge held if you lifted or charged any of the characters from back then – they would take their punishment and move on. He could remember being called out to a massive brawl in the middle of the Crescent with at least a dozen men kicking hell out of each other with baseball bats and other less sporting items.

On that occasion discretion was used. After sitting in the police van for ten minutes the coppers decided to go back to the station for a cup of tea and a fag, returning about half-an-hour later to pick up the pieces, including baseball bats, chair legs, and iron bars, in between the walking wounded and advising the protagonists it would be a good idea to *'get hame'*. If this was to happen now there would be half-a-dozen police vans, the SWAT squad, a police helicopter, and a mountain of paper work. The retired policeman's parting shot was that it looked like a twentieth-century version of the *Battle of the Clans*. He also fondly remembered all the big families and characters including Tin Ligs McGoldrick, Pony Williamson, and Blondie Dow.

You never quite forget the smell of charred furniture lying at the front of a house that had been ablaze the night before – still smouldering as you walked to school. At one stage in the late 1970s and throughout the 1980s there was an epidemic of house fires, many started deliberately in the hope that the house would be so badly damaged the family would be moved out of the housing scheme. Mostly the family was moved to another house elsewhere in the Crescent. If there had been fire-alarms fitted to every house in Hunters the estate would have sounded like a 1990s rave.

Hunter Crescent must have been a close second to London during the blitz for buildings on fire. It is beyond me why the fire brigade did not have a sub-station in the middle of the housing scheme. Winter seemed to be the busiest period. Typically you would hear the sirens of the fire engines speeding into Hunters followed by the call of so-and-so's *'lum was up'*. You would usually see sparks and flames licking out the top of the chimney. This was caused by people not having their chimney cleaned or by some of the items placed onto the fire to generate heat. It was not always coal, wood, or other solid fuels that were used: club books, old clothes and even old shoes – they tell me you could get a braw heat off a pair of platform boots! Some people would have a gas fire or a three-bar electric fire but they were the elite in Hunters.

Coal fires were archaic in many ways. If you wanted a bath, you had to put the blower on for a couple hours, which meant fiddling about with the poker half way up the chimney to open a vent in the lum to heat water. If you wanted a bath your mum would say:

'I'll put the blower on for you'.

This would give you half a bath full of water that would be topped up with boiling pots of water. You still had to share a bath with your brothers and sisters. Failing that it was a wash in the kitchen sink. Even at a tender age of six it was embarrassing having your winkie washed as the 1744 Perth to Inverness train went hurtling pass the window just fifty yards away.

One winter our neighbour who was a right character had decided to do a bit of interior design and painted the brickwork in her fireplace with gloss paint. The next evening her man Willie lit the fire and it didn't take long to heat the room, the flat, even the entire close. I can vaguely remember my mum saying:

'*Christ it's like an oven in here*'

as right on queue there was a frantic chap at the door.

It was Helen from down the stairs crying that she had '*set fire tae ma hoose*'. I think it took about three fire engines to put the fire out. It was always a mystery who phoned them, as for all the years I stayed there the only people I knew that were wealthy enough to have a phone in the house were Evelyn and Ian McCullie.

Bonfire/Guy Fawkes night was like a national holiday in Hunters. Gangs would plan for weeks and build fires that would put the one in *The Wicker Man* to shame. Fundraising involved going around with a Guy in an old pram asking for '*a penny for the guy*'. Incidentally the Guy was usually better dressed than the crew pushing the pram around and I often wondered where the collected pennies went as they didn't need to buy firewood.

Guising was a money-making opportunity for youthful entrepreneurs. You would dress up in old clothes and be an old tramp or use an old bed-sheet with holes in it to turn you into a ghost. Some would splash out and buy a 25p plastic witch mask and a black bag to be used as a cape. Not like now where it is '*Trick or Treat*' and supermarkets sell overpriced outfits in July – three months before the event. We used our imagination.

Kids now just turn up at the door with puppy-dog eyes expecting money or treats. We had to learn a song or a joke. We even pushed the boat out and carved a face into a neep to make a scary face. Unlike the fancy pumpkins you see in American horror films, however, a neep is made of stronger stuff, and by the time you had cored it out and cut a face into its skin it looked more like a skeleton that had had a stroke.

Unfortunately things could and did go wrong on Guy Fawkes Night. Building bonfires next to the wall of a house is never a good idea nor is throwing on empty gas-bottles or car tyres full of air. They would take-off like missiles when they reached a certain temperature.

Another culprit for a Hunters house fire was the good old chip pan.

No one has a chip pan now. You would probably have to go to the museum up George Street or watch an episode of *Antiques Roadshow* to see one but back in the 1970s and 1980s they were a mainstay of the kitchen – most things would be deep fried, even lettuce.

The usual scenario would be for someone to come home boozy, peel some chips, stick the chip pan on, sit down in the living room, fall asleep, then wake up blacked-up like Al Jolson in an ambulance receiving oxygen. People don't get boozy anymore. It's not trendy but they did in the 1970s and 1980s. Now you get bladdered, rubbered, or wrecked but not boozy.

House fires would leave closes in a real mess, all fire damaged and smelling of smoke – and it seemed the council were in no rush to do repairs and it could take months to put things right – yet again leaving the people of Hunter Crescent thinking no one was interested in helping them. As we moved into the 1980s the council did fewer and fewer repairs – houses were boarded up with corrugated iron. Some of the blocks had five empty boarded-up flats with just a single tenant in one property.

On the rare occasion an ambulance came into Hunter Crescent it would usually ghost in without a sound, no siren blasting. Nonetheless, all the local gossips, fishwives, and soothsayers would be at the window within seconds – it was almost like they had in-built radar that alerted them. They would be at the bottom of their stairs gathering in twos and threes muttering:

'Her man's no been weel for weeks',

'Bet it's a heart attack',

or

'She's deed'.

Not one of them was medically qualified but nine times out of ten their diagnosis would be correct. You would also get people walking past the ambulance scene as if they were walking in mud up to their waist just to get a view of what was happening.

There was also an occasion when the local council dogcatcher and several policeman came in to do the yearly cull of dogs in Hunter Crescent. The breeds of dog that went around the Crescent in packs, scavenging in bins, chasing cars, and fighting each other were not, and never will, be the breeds you see at Crufts. You could get a Golden Retriever cross Chihuahua, a Greyhound cross Pug, or even a Pit Bull cross Poodle.

The dogcatcher in his shiny suit and peaked cap didn't look any older than us. As he trapped about seven dogs in the corner of the park he swung his long pole with a net on it into the snarling pile of fur, teeth, and fleas, managing to catch the smallest one. From that point it all went wrong. First the other dogs pulled him to the ground and although he eventually got back on his feet, his trousers were ripped, his sleeve was hanging off, and his peaked cap a distant memory. I vaguely remember Gaynor McLean, Yvonne Grant, Erica Frampton, a few others, and myself laughing our heads off from our vantage point at the top of a climbing frame. The poor guy looked up at us and shouted something like:

'*Yer aw a bunch a ***** animals, think it's funny aye?*'

then just launched the pole into one of the overgrown gardens never to be seen again.

As well as packs of dogs there were plenty of cats but the *Best Pet in Hunters* prize goes to the Lackies who had a pet goose that lived in their back garden but wandered round the Crescent like it owned it. He was a moody bugger. Depending on what mood he was in he would eat bread out your hand or chase you down the street hissing and flapping his wings. Even the local wild dog packs avoided upsetting it – though I think Hunters' very own *Goosey Goosey Gander's* demise involved a dog.

One law that didn't come under the jurisdiction of any Scottish court was Parents Law. I got all the usual punishments: slapped with a slipper; a clip round the legs; and a slap on the back of the head. What astounded me was the memory of my mum. She would be washing my hair at the sink and she would say:

'*Now I asked you to go to the shop on Tuesday at 4:33 pm and I heard you swearing in the close when you went out*'.

This was generally followed by slap-slap on the back of the neck. You had no offer of a lawyer and the sentence was swift.

As you got older it didn't work. You would be laughing at the contorted look on you mum's face as she was swinging the slipper at you. The only punishment that worked then was to be grounded, which *was* a punishment. We didn't have what the kids have today. Being sent to your room back then *was* a punishment. I didn't have all the mod cons of today in my room. I had only a wee portable black and white television.

The worst ever sentence was when I had a hissy fit about having to go and bring the washing in, doing the dead-fly dance on the kitchen floor pointing to my brother and pleading:

'*Why me?*'

and

'*How no him?*'.

I had a big semi-final to play for a new team, North Inch Rovers, and I didn't have time for women's work. Just like that she snapped. I was grounded and going nowhere. I quickly changed my tune and went and got the washing but there was no budging her. I even tried for a suspended sentence asking if I could just '*nip out*' for a couple of hours to play the game but it was a '*no*'. Giving up I was left thinking I bet Peter Shilton didn't have these problems.

These were the standard punishments most Hunters kids would have been served. I have seen another side of this where some parents took it to a different level. I remember one boy being beaten up in the park by his dad for taking a biscuit without asking. This was a full-grown man beating up a boy of maybe twelve. At one stage he picked him up and threw him onto the concrete. He landed on the back of his hand, four of his knuckles shoved halfway up the back of his hand. The boy was screaming. His dad just grabbed him and pushed them back into position, every one of them making a clicking sound as they were popped back into position, ranting:

'*Why you screaming? There's nothing wrong with you*'.

In the main most Hunters kids knew right from wrong and had a good upbringing but that's not to say there weren't a few wild buggers.

Photographs

1

Hunter Crescent, possibly 1940s
At 18 Hunter Crescent, possibly c1964

Hunters' first boy band – Eddie Frampton, Alex Williamson
and Fareed Tanyous, late 1980s
'Hunters Own', the Punk Era

Ruthven Place
Feus Hoose, 1958

Feus Hoose, early 1980s
Tollhoose Stores (Scott's), 1980s

Community House *(Polaroid print)*
Ruthven Avenue, 1980s
Opposite: Cappy Oswald

Cappy Oswald and Roxanne Fraser, local community worker
Kung Fu Willie *(centre)*
Opposite: Jean Rattray *(front centre)*

John Lees, ticky-man

Jimmy Horn, ticky-man
The Hool, Dave Hoolachan *(centre)*

Eddie Frampton, local entrepreneur

Brian Morrison

CHAPTER FOUR

Away for the Messages

NO ONLINE SHOPPING, no twenty-four-hour shopping, nor home delivery and you would struggle to find what we call a supermarket today but what we had in Hunters was a choice of shops, door-to-door salesmen, and mobile shops that seemed endless.

One of the most popular shops with the good people of Hunters was Scott's paper shop that was owned by Enid Cavellini and her man Jimmy. No matter what time of day you went in it was busy. It was very much in the style of the shop in *Open All Hours*: floor to ceiling wooden shelves neatly stacked with all sorts of retail delights, from jars of coffee to tins of ham and soap powder, and everything in between. The main counter was an old wooden worktop that had a freezer underneath with a slide top on it storing the usual staples: fish fingers, frozen chips, ice poles, frozen Kwenchy Kups, and for the lucky few, blocks of ice cream that you could ask to be cut in half if you couldn't afford the full thing. There were usually two or three clear plastic cake displays on the counter. They used to sell a trifle for about 12p. To this day I have never found a better one. Also, there would be a hill of McIntyre's fresh rolls. They were a delicacy on a Saturday morning in our house. They would be complemented with this tasty butter that was rounded in shape and covered in either red or green paper.

Behind the counter there was a display of chocolate bars and sweets I still hanker for today: Texan Bars, Spangles, Curly Wurlies (when they were the length of your arm) Bar Six, Five Centres, and Golden Cups – the list could go on and on. Above that, you had every type of cigarette you could wish to fill your lungs with.

Talking of cigarettes – Enid always had a fag in her mouth while serving. She could be cutting you four slices of chopped pork, or cutting you some cheese, or handling cakes – we all survived. It's hard to believe that back then children could buy cigarettes if their parents sent them to the shop for them, no questions asked. A different time but some shops would also sell them to kids as singles or fives, and put them in a sweetie bag for you. Now if you look underage you need a birth certificate, passport, and a letter from your bank to buy them.

The other half of the shop was a newsagent and it was run by Jimmy who was a chubby wee man with a purple nose. He wore a grey shop jacket you'd never see today. Everything was behind a grill with magazines behind it. The newspapers were placed on the top. You could also get a football coupon and *'something for the weekend'*. It was a hub of activity around seven o'clock on a Saturday night. At that time a van would appear and throw a pile of *'Sporting Posts'* out the window. Some kid would run into the shop with the papers and an army of men who had been loitering outside would bolt into the shop like whippets to check their pools coupons:

'Checking the results in the Post'.

Within minutes industrial language would fill the air and the dream would have to wait till next week.

The Cavallini family also owned the chippy next door that went like a fair. I have never forgotten the display behind the counter of large glass bottles of TC soft drinks alongside Lilt, Coca Cola (which were the large fancy bottles you only see in the small bottles now), and Fanta – and all the glass jars of sweets in the corner: kola cubes, pineapple chunks, chewing nuts, and lemon bonbons, just to mention a few.

One thing that used to annoy me in the chippy was standing in a long queue waiting to get served and some half-cut old guy in a blazer with a purple nose (with a giant British Legion badge on his chest pocket) staggering in after a few too many Black and Tans and shouting:

'Throw in a fish and a black pudding Enid!'.

The reply was usually:

'Aye love nae problem'.

A few weeks later, I thought I would try this method, saying:

'Throw in a white pudding Enid'.

I didn't quite get the answer I was expecting. She peered over the fryer, gave me the death stare, which all wee wifies are trained in, and shouted:

'You'll wait yer turn, ya cheeky wee bugger!'.

Two hundred yards up the Crieff Road there was a post office/ greengrocers called Hearn's, run by two brothers John and Gary whose family had started the business back in 1939. It was a lovely shop. It had a smell you don't get in shops anymore – it was a smell of sweets, fruit and veg, and a hint of coffee. Everything was behind the counter, stacked neatly and all facing the right way. Staff were always cheery. In fact Gary Hearn had his own wee catch phrase. When he was giving you your change, he would go *'boom-boom'* for no apparent reason. The other half of the shop was a post office – a proper post office with the old weights, chains with a pen attached, old ledgers behind the glass counter, and big books of stamps, I used to get sent along to get the family allowance. John would stamp the book and give you it back with cash.

It's funny how you remember stupid things from almost forty years ago. I remember my mum giving me a message line to go to Hearn's for milk, bread, and Dr Whites. Gary put the bread and milk on the counter and then looked at the note, then at me, and said:

'What size of Dr White's?'.

Like I knew what I was talking about I said:

'Large please'.

It is pleasing to note that the lane down the side of the old post office is today still known as Hearn's Lane as it was back in the good old days. I just wish it had a street sign telling people that.

Todd's greengrocery was another shop at the top of the Crescent directly across from Feus Road. It is now a car stereo shop. I don't think it was as busy as the other two shops. Todd's, run by a Mr Todd strangely enough, was your typical grocers shop of its time. I can still recall going in and Mr Todd would tuck in his thumb saying he cut it off on the meat slicer.

That was it then: three shops all within 500 yards of each other all making a decent living.

They all ran ticky books. You would settle-up on Friday and if you didn't your name went on a list and was posted in the window. By the same token, if you were 10p short, they would say:

'Hand it in tomorrow'.

Can you imagine a big supermarket saying that? Those shops were all a big part of the community and the daily life of Hunter Crescent.

Further afield, across the Crieff Road bridge, you had a Co-operative Society store and a paper shop – I think it was called Linens – run by a man and wife. He was tall and grey. The wife was a dumpy woman with a tight perm and Deirdre Barlow glasses. The minute you walked into shop to buy a 10p mix all you got was:

'Hurry up I've not got all day'.

It was like we were pariahs. They were embarrassed to have us in the shop … but happy to take our money. It was a typical shop of its time with small bags of coal, kindling, and fruit and vegetables outside.

If you couldn't be bothered leaving the Crescent that was okay as the choice of mobile shops was plentiful. Most of us would have got our coal delivered by Cappy Oswald, a tiny wee man with a weathered face and filthy black flat cap. You would hear him coming as he had a leather money bag that would jingle as he walked. Jimmy Fairlie was his right-hand coalman and took over from Cappy when he retired. Jimmy was a great guy who always had time for a laugh and a joke. Another coal supplier was Fenton's. All these coalmen must have had some upper body strength. They could lift a hundredweight (over eight stone) up two or three flights of stairs without leaving a mess as they delivered the coal into your coal bunker at the end of the hall.

If you were feeling flush, you could buy coal nuts or briquettes, or logs from Andy Windgate. (In the early 1980s the *'Perthshire Advertiser'* ran a story in which it was claimed the council was refusing to continually replace close doors as they suspected they were being chopped up and used for firewood – Andy's sales may have taken a drop then!)

On a Friday you would have the fish van and as we were Catholic the Friday dinner choice was fish, fish, or fish. Crawfords' bakery van used to come into the Crescent – I suspect at the end of their shift – selling broken cakes or short dated cakes. Bill Payne was the baker at the time. There were others but Bill was the one I remember. I recall he used to take pity on us and give us broken meringues for nothing.

I got to know Bill later in life. He has a great character with a brilliant sense of humour. Anytime I would see him in town he would say if you are ever looking for a cheap Rolex, fags, even machine guns, I can get them, *'wink-wink'*.

Other grocery vans that did a roaring trade included Jock Tripney's (technically his was a converted bus crammed with stock), Dino's, McLaren's, Jimmy Miller's, and Frank Morrow's (with *'Come to Morrow's Today'* emblazoned on the side). Inglis ran another grocery van. With his slicked back hair he looked like the love child of Dracula and Ray Reardon. I remember in the winter he would have a gas heater on wheels behind the counter while he smoked a fag next to it. He was just a mobile explosion waiting to happen.

Ice cream vans were ten a penny but the only one I can remember was Sergio Cura's. He had continued the business when his dad Dino retired. I recall him getting a new purple ice cream van and Willie Burns and me jumping on the back of it. The plan was to jump off as it left the Crescent. Unfortunately for me I got my baseball boots stuck under the back door of the van as it turned left onto the Crieff Road with the faint sound of Willie laughing at the shocked look on my face as I struggled to get free. By the time the van was speeding over the Crieff Road bridge I knew I was in trouble. Then, as Sergio put his foot down as he headed down the A9 to Bankfoot, cars were passing us on the outside lane and I was giving them an embarrassing nod as they went past – some were even peeping to get Sergio's attention but he must have had the radio on loud. Just as we got into Bankfoot I managed to get loose and jumped off the back. It's a long nine-mile walk from Bankfoot to Hunter Crescent.

Mention the name of Italian legend Piccolino to anyone from

Hunters and they will automatically think of toffee apples and puff candy. You would hear him first, blowing his whistle like he was at a rave. It was a sight never to be forgotten: a man dressed in a railway jacket and hat (that was his day job, I think he was a signalman for British Rail) on a push bike with a plastic box tied to the front and carrier bags for collecting empty bottles, which were the unofficial currency of Hunters, blowing the whistle and shouting:

'Toffee apples – come and a getta puffa a candy!'.

He would also say:

'Finda me twenty lolly sticks, I give you free puff candy'.

He was way ahead of everyone when it came to being ecofriendly and saving the planet as he would pick up dirty lolly sticks and re-use them – without washing them. Sometimes when he was drunk he would be trying to sell his merchandise at eleven at night. You would hear the whistle and the silhouette of a man on a bike swaying from one side of the road to the other. He didn't always have a bike. He sometimes used a tiny van but every time he came in to Hunters with the vehicle gangs would start rocking the van and almost tip it over – it was like a scene from a western with the Apaches trying to turn a wagon over. Piccolino would spoil the illusion by shouting in Italian:

'Affanculo bastardy'.

There was also a paper van that St Johnstone legend Willie Coburn drove that used to come around on a Sunday selling newspapers, rolls, and scratchcards – before there were scratchcards. They were like a wee window in an advent calendar. I remember my dad winning £40, which seemed like a fortune back then.

Also you would get the ragman every so often. That was a very simple transaction. You gave him old clothes and in return you got a gobstopper, a bouncy ball, a balloon, or a goldfish … only problem was some kids took their dad's Sunday suit (I say Sunday suit, it was more than likely their suit for wearing when they had to go to court) or their mum's wedding dress. It was also common practice for people to have their washing stolen (commonly known as snow dropping) and sold to the ragman.

You would have your door-to-door salesmen. These varied from the legitimate salesman selling cleaning goods from a suitcase to the shady characters who would turn up at the door selling things like rolls of carpets, television sets, cutlery, and ten gallons of black paint. My favourite salesman and probably the *hardest* was the Indian gent that used to offer to sharpen your knives and scissors – how hard is that? Walking into Hunters and yup I know this is a rough area but I'll sharpen your knives and scissors – if you have an axe or shears, I can sharpen that too! He also had a catch phrase:

'*Lucky beans, lucky beans*',

which you would be given after he had done his deed.

Ticky-men were feared but a necessity in Hunter Crescent. There are three companies I remember: Sloan's, Household, and Provident. Sloan's, the ticky-man for them was John Lees, a smartly dressed wee man who always wore a hat – either a trilby or in the winter a flat cap. At Christmas we would get a box of Quality Street for being a good customer. He would usually come on a Friday night and he and my dad would discuss the bets for Saturday at Kempton Park, Sandown, and Ascot. (I keep in touch with his daughter Paula and she tells me he is enjoying retirement. He is a great-grandad now and recently celebrated his eightieth birthday.)

Household were the other company that would come to the house. Jimmy Horn was their collector. Jimmy was a brilliant guy, always had a joke, and sometimes a song – usually a Frank Sinatra or Dean Martin number. He also did a wee comedy act. If you couldn't pay and had a sad tale of how you couldn't pay he would pull out a hanky and hand it to you with a straight face. But he was a decent guy and understood people were struggling on not a lot of money. Jimmy has retired now and is living out his retirement in Fairfield.

These two businesses had shops in the town centre. Household were situated in South Street and Sloan's in the old High Street – their shop a throwback to a department store of the 1950s, with glass counters and drawers underneath with socks, ties, and shirts, even cufflinks, all that was missing was someone shouting:

'*I'm free!*'.

Household were slightly more modern. I used to get my maroon Waffle Stay Press and Monkey Boots from there. These were shops where you would go in, pick the goods you required, which you would get on credit recorded in a ledger, and you would pay weekly to the ticky-man.

The third ticky-man was Mr Scott. He was a total gent, was always very dapper in a check jacket, shirt and tie, and he had the Golden Ticket, otherwise known as a Provy Cheque. You would ask Mr Scott for a loan and he would give you what I can only describe as a small book with carbon paper in it. When you spent it in a shop they would write down how much you had spent and what you had left. To find who took a Provy Cheque, you had to look for a discreet sticker in a shop window saying:

'*Provident Cheques Accepted*'.

You were limited in Perth. You had Bennies, Drummond's, a fashion store called Satisfaction Guaranteed, one or two others but the major store was Woolworths, as my brother John will confirm. He must have been about eleven when he was given a £20 Provy Cheque to spend. He was going through his farming stage and was mad on Britain Toy Tractors. He bought a couple of tractors, a couple of sheep, and a plough, handing the goods over at the counter with the Provy Cheque. The assistant bagged his toys and gave him the Provy Cheque back with 99p left, as they wouldn't give you cash if there was something remaining on the cheque. Now John has never liked wasting money and spent an hour looking for something to spend his 99p on. Eventually, he found a family sized bag of dry roasted peanuts. He handed them over to the shop assistant who cheerily went:

'*That's 99p please*'.

John slid the Provy Cheque over the counter. The assistant quickly changed her tune and in disgust said:

'*Provy cheque for a packet of peanuts?*'.

To which John replied in a deadpan voice:

'*It's legal tender*'.

These loan/payment companies were used by a high percentage

of the families in Hunter Crescent and could be a godsend if your cooker or fridge broke down as very few would have money sitting about to replace them.

Occasionally when money was tight and you couldn't afford your weekly payment, the door would be locked, the telly and lights turned off, and just to be safe you'd hide behind the couch, which was pointless unless the ticky-man had a periscope or a neck like a giraffe as we lived on the first floor. It was a game of cat-and-mouse. You would hear the chap, your heart would be pounding, then a deadly silence, no one would move, you could hear a fly fart, then as you thought the ticky-man had gone, he would bluff you and chap again sending family members in all directions like a grenade had just gone off. Other families would send a child to the door to say:

'Dad's not in'.

Sometimes they'd fail and say:

'My mum says she's not in'.

At the end of the day they were all seen as friends and as I said earlier, a godsend at a time when money was hard to come by – and are fondly remembered today.

CHAPTER FIVE

Hunters Legends

IN FEBRUARY 2016 I had the honour of an audience with the Queen of Hunter Crescent. The minute I got to her house I was made very welcome:

'Sit doon son do you want a cup of tea?'.

Considering what Alice Mcguire has done for Hunters she is a very modest lady. Alice has lived in the same house, 43C Hunter Crescent, since 1946, living there with her mum and dad, Trevor and Judy, and later bringing up her own family there. When I asked as to her favourite time in Hunter Crescent she answered without hesitation:

'The 1950s and 1960s were a brilliant time'.

She recalled all the house parties that would go on for days, the big street party they had for the Queen's coronation. She also remembered the great excitement of one of her neighbours in Hunters getting the first television on the estate and without batting an eyelid pointed to a close in the distance and said:

'Aye it was the Lackies that lived at 26'.

About the people and times she missed, she talked fondly of characters like Tin Ligs McGoldrick, Shuggie Williamson, Kung Fu Willie, Jake Sinclair, the Hool, and many, many others – all of them legends and everyone who lived in the Crescent will remember them as *'well kent faces'*.

Shuggie Williamson was well known for running tattie and berry vans and buses in the summer and autumn that left the Crescent early in the morning. He moved to Perth in the 1960s after meeting Maureen, his wife-to-be. He was working at fairgrounds all over Scotland but the Paisley native decided to make Perth his home. What a lot of people will not know is that Shuggie saved someone's life back in 1978. After a night on the town he noticed a neighbour across the road struggling to get out of their ground floor flat that was on fire. He managed to get the man out of the window before the emergency services arrived.

Jake Sinclair did a lot for the youth of Hunter Crescent and had a big say in the community tin huts brought to the *Dump* – along with Bob Smith, Councillor Stewart, Miss Dempsey, and Nicky McLean who helped with their construction and many more people in Hunter Crescent. The *Tin Hut* goes down in history with people of my age for its discos, jumble sales, playgroups, and Christmas parties. It was the hub for the youth of Hunter Crescent. When you walked in there was a mural on the wall with a tree painted on it called the *Tree of Dignity*. Situated on the edge of the *Dump* it eventually fell into disrepair due to issues with the floor.

Kung Fu Willie was a gem of a guy who, as his name suggests, was a martial arts expert and could probably snap you in two with his fingers. He was, however, one of the nicest guys you could meet. He was also a bit of a local star as he starred in a BBC drama called *The Mad Death,* which I think was about rabies. I can remember the streets of Hunters being deserted as everyone went home to watch Willie's ten seconds of fame, dressed as a soldier in the woods looking for wild dogs. It was a big deal. One of our own was on the television ... and it wasn't for a court case or some other misdemeanour on the news.

I only saw Kung Fu Willie in action once – think I was about ten. There was about a half-dozen of us playing football in the park when some adults decided to take the football off us. Willie had been passing through and asked them to *'leave the bairns alane'*. Two of them recognised Kung Fu Willie and took his advice but the third one must have been on *brave pills* and decided to take Willie on ... ten seconds later it was all over with Willie putting on some kind of armlock and the would-be hard man yelping like a dog. As they ran off one of the adults shouted:

'Don't fuck with the Fu!'.

He was a well-respected doorman for a lot of the pubs and clubs in Perth for many years – a decent guy who sadly passed away too soon.

The Hool (Davie Hoolachan) was a giant of a man in stature and personality. He always had a word for everybody and was always laughing and joking. Many a time he would be passing through the park on his way to cut somebody's grass and he would stop and join in with a game of football. The Hool worked in the *Feus Hoose* at one time as I can remember him throwing three drunks out of the pub like they were rag dolls. He was also one of the godfathers of the tattie squads, running a van during tattie-picking season.

In the summer he was kept busy cutting the back greens in the Crescent, a full-time job for one man. He had also served in the Scots Guards and was a highly regarded boxer. Numerous people who saw him box said he could have gone pro. Anytime he would see my dad he would say *'Maltese Lace'*, after my dad had given it to him as a tip on numerous occasions without the useless horse ever winning. He always had a bottle of cola in his pocket and, just like Kung Fu Willie, died too young.

Davie Seaton was a Hunters legend to the generations who grew up in the 1980s and 1990s. He was well known round town for selling the *Evening Telegraph* and *Sporting Post*. Dave would also frequent the pubs and nightclubs trying to sell you a newspaper as you were trying to chat up some lady in the dim light of the *York House* (the *Yorkie*), Perth's premier nightclub at the time. He would pester you till you bought one. I would counter this occasionally by telling him some poor woman on the dancefloor fancied him. He would then pester her for the rest of the night and I would save myself 25p.

Davie was a big footy fan but had no loyalties to any one club. Once a team lost form he would jump ship: St Johnstone, Glasgow Rangers, Dundee United, Raith Rovers, and Inverness Caledonian Thistle, to name a few of his abandoned clubs. It maybe an urban myth but I remember a story doing the rounds in the late 1980s in which the local football casuals felt sorry for him and bought him a load of designer gear to smarten him up, only for him to sell them all a few days later. Knowing the Perth casuals were after him he went into hiding with relatives, possibly in Dundee.

Davie was also a magician of David Copperfield proportions.

On 5 October 1988, my dad, my brother, and I decided to go through to see Dundee United play Maltese team Floriana FC in a European Cup Winners' Cup game. We got on the train from Perth – one of the old type with compartments and a sliding door – and as the train pulled out Davie (who was supporting United in 1988) joined us. He decided to take a nap and lay down, taking his shoes off before getting comfy. His feet and shoes were stinking and I mean turn your guts stinking. As he fell asleep we decided to throw his trainers out the window. In throwing out his trainers we didn't give a second thought to the decimation the smell may cause to a herd of livestock grazing in the fields. When the train pulled into Dundee station we got off before he could question us. The next we saw of him was at Tannadice with a shiny pair of brogues on – this was before late night shopping. Where did he get the shoes?

Don Stewart, the bookie, is also fondly remembered by some of the older Hunter Crescent gang. The Stewarts were a large family and lived at 16 Ruthven Avenue. Don's runner was a chap called Stan Cruickshanks. Most housing schemes had a resident bookie's runner. For the uninformed a bookie's runner was a gent who would collect bets from punters in housing schemes and deliver them to a bookmaker, for what I would imagine a small commission. That time was a lifetime away from the online bookmaking of today or every town being overrun by bookmaker shops. (Perth has nine at last count. When growing up, I think there were two or three.)

Don would hire two or three buses every so often (during the summer months) to take the men to the races at Ayr or Musselburgh. All the kids and mums would be taken to the beach with picnics. He supplied the crisps, drinks, and sandwiches for the day-trippers.

At my end of the Crescent the bookie's runner was Max Donaldson who collected bets for Henry Giulianotti, a local bookmaker and publican. Occasionally I would be sent to his flat with a piece of paper from my dad with horses' names on it followed by all sorts of permutations: 6 x 10p doubles; 4 x 10p trebles; and a 20p roll-up.

Many people will remember Eric the Pole. He was Hunters' version of Cash Convertors. A sort of pawnbroker, Eric would buy almost anything from gold and silver, to clocks, shoes, and televisions. I can remember my dad going round one time to buy a transistor radio. When we went round to Eric's house at Ruthven Avenue we were invited into the kitchen where we squeezed past a ton of other stuff in the kitchen. He had more radios for sale than Currys – all makes and models. The rest of the house was much the same. It was like the set from *Steptoe and Son* with stacks of goods your eyes couldn't quite take in – piles of kettles, bike wheels, lawn mowers, and everything else in between. I think my dad came out with a big 1950s radio and a puncture repair kit (and he didn't even own a bike).

Jewellery and watch repairs were another of Eric's skills. Eric was also an Edward Scissorhands offering cheap haircuts. I think there were two choices: skinhead or bowl cut, for not much more than 50p. I vaguely remember one transaction with Eric. I'd found a carrier bag of Embassy Cigarettes coupons up at Ten Talls while heading back from my cousins in Hillyland. Eric paid me £3 cash muttering something in broken English about *'no be easy to get rid of'*. To those who don't remember them, Embassy would put in approximately five coupons per packet, so after you had smoked about 800 fags, you had enough coupons to exchange for a bedside lamp or an umbrella – not forgetting an iron lung.

Alice Mcguire also spoke about a woman called Mrs Christie who would turn up at your house to see if your close and house were tidy and it always seemed to be at a time people were having their tea and on numerous occasions Alice's mum would chase her out the house with a rolling pin. Alice recalled her neighbour Johnny McFarlane who would take his two pet donkeys into the close to feed them.

Alice's own memories include helping to run the famous *Tin Hut*. There were also days out such as the bus trips to Bucky Braes. Alice reminded me of an incident when a convoy of three buses from Hunters went to Arbroath for the day. Everyone had a great day but on the return home Kenny Leaver wasn't on the bus. We didn't realise he was missing till we passed Dundee, so we turned back. When we found him he was sitting in the police station eating biscuits.

Laughing out loud, Alice told me that she said:

'*Never mind the biscuits git yer arse on the bus*'.

Jean Rattray is a Perth legend, let alone a Hunters legend. She had a house in Ruthven Avenue but to be honest, I can hardly remember seeing her in the sixteen years I stayed in the Crescent. There were a great many stories about her, most in my opinion urban myths. What I was told about Jean I took with a pinch of salt:

'*Yeah, her parents were millionaires*',

'*She was a university lecturer*',

and

'*Her boyfriend was a pilot who died in a plane crash*'.

What I do know is that underneath the brazen, shouting Jean, there was another side. I remember her asking me for 20p for a can of lager. I gave her 40p and said '*get me one as well*'. Her retort was:

'*Ah ya cheeky bastard ... thanks darling*'.

Whatever the reason something turned her to alcoholism, which is a disease – something people sometimes overlook. She could be a pain in the arse (just like the rest of us) but she was harmless. She wasn't a bad person, just made some bad choices in life. She died in her fifties. The Salvation Army organised Jean's funeral to which there was a large turnout. A large collection of bouquets of flowers were left at her favourite haunt outside the old post office in South Street but the most poignant item left was an unopened can of Carlsberg lager.

The community flat in Ruthven Avenue where adults and children could go for advice and classes was a hub of activity. Many Hunter Crescent residents used the centre to make phone-calls or have a letter read and typed up. The community flat was run by Basil Smith and Edith Kift, man and wife who moved to the Perthshire area in the early 1970s – and as already mentioned, a couple fondly remembered by former Hunter Crescent residents.

Basil was the senior community social worker. He was quite distinctive with his hair standing on end and a pipe in his mouth. He also drove a big Volvo. Basil could wind people up but he had great plans for the housing estate and had a kind heart and always looked out for the interests of the people of Hunters. Edith was very highly regarded in Hunter Crescent and seemed to be able to identify with the social issues the residents were dealing with on a daily basis. She was a shoulder to cry on, an agony aunt to many of the residents, and helped with a range of needs from reading letters to letting people use the office phone.

Alice thought that as the 1970s came in, the council were giving up on Hunters and stopped spending money on repairs. Even the police treated it like a no-go zone. Alice could see the housing scheme going downhill rapidly. All the new changes had not worked and the place looked run down. In the mid-1980s the council all but condemned it but the architects told them the buildings were well constructed and could be regenerated. Alice and other tenants got together and with the backing of local councillors such as Davy Scott and city factor Gerry Black and support at weekly meetings from Drew Mackie Associates and Gaia Architects, Fairfield took shape. At the first meeting with the council, Alice told them:

'Speak oor language, no that gobbledegook'.

Some tenants seemed against the development and there was a bit of negativity from them. Then when Number 39 was finished, an open day was organised, which included entertainment from the Vale of Atholl Pipe Band with Pipe Major Ian Duncan. After tenants had the chance to have a look around the block of refurbished flats eighty-two people expressed an interest in renting one of the Fairfield properties.

Alice Mcguire is the most unassuming person you could ever meet and when I asked her about being awarded the MBE (she told me it stands for *'More Bottles Empty'*) – it was like it was nothing. She had to dig it out of a drawer for me. It was in a beautiful box but not on display. The day she found out she was to receive the award Alice thought it was a wind up. She had just got home and the phone rang. It was Brigadier Charlie Grant from the Territorial Army who told her. She couldn't believe it. In fact she thought it was a prank and put the phone down. She ran into the street and told Mark Paddick who also thought it was a wind up. After she had returned home the phone rang again and this time the brigadier convinced her it was true. Her son and daughter, Trevor and Judy, were sworn to secrecy for six weeks before it was announced officially.

With the announcement Alice was inundated by the press (on the phone and at the door) because she had been awarded the MBE for services to Fairfield and the Territorial Army. She was given her MBE by Prince Charles who spoke to her for ten minutes instead of the regular four. The only disappointment was the catering. Alice was expecting a banquet but everyone who was being awarded that day were given bottled water and tea biscuits. When the story appeared in the local press no one could believe it. And as Alice says:

'Och, it was a great thing – no one from Hunters or Fairfield have had this … I was pissed for three weeks'.

As much as Alice loves how Fairfield has turned out – with full occupancy and a long waiting list it is no longer a place where people do not want to live and there is not a stigma about living there as there was all those years ago – she laments the loss of the community spirit and characters it had back in the good old days.

CHAPTER SIX

Teach Yourself Eggy

ONE THING I found surprising was Alice did not speak *Eggy*, the national language of Hunter Crescent – the language of the people. Incidentally the first time I heard *Eggy* was at a wedding scramble around the other end of the Crescent, next door to where Alice lived. (Wedding scrambles seemed to be a custom of the 1970s and 1980s. You don't see them today.)

The father came out the close with the blushing bride. The locals then showered them with confetti. As the dad got in the car and it drove off, the window was opened and a shower of coins was thrown out – mostly brown coins (one and two pences) with the odd silver coin (five or ten pences). At this stage, the local kids acted like a school of piranha fish fighting over somebody's leg. Diving on the pavement, pushing, scratching, and biting to get the illusive silver coins. As I spotted a ten pence piece rolling in my direction, a rough looking kid barged me out the way and said:

'*Fegguck eggoff theggat's meggine*',

which loosely translates as

'Excuse me young chap, I think you'll find that coin is mine'.

It didn't take me long to master the art of *Eggy*. After all, in order to spend the next ten years in that concrete jungle, I would need it to survive.

For years I thought *Eggy* was a language only spoken in Hunter Crescent. Once I started researching the language on the internet I found out there were other housing schemes where the language was spoken – and *Eggy* has been studied by university professors. One professor of languages described *Eggy* as a secret language rather like pig Latin and cockney rhyming slang. *Eggy* can take a while to master but once taught it can be used for private conversation with little chance of others understanding the conversation. It can be

68

taught and understood very rapidly but is nonetheless unintelligible to the untrained ear.

My research uncovered a murder in Northfield, Aberdeen, where in the subsequent court case the judge asked a policeman what the accused said when he arrested him to which the policeman replied:

'I could not understand him your honour as he spoke in a language called Eggy'.

I also came across the story of a serial shoplifter in Edinburgh who was caught by the police leaving a Tesco superstore and charged with shoplifting and breach of the peace for calling the two officers a couple of *'beggacon reggolls'*. In court, the judge asked one of the police officers what this meant to which he replied:

'A couple of bacon rolls',

a common insult used against the police.

When the judge asked him how he understood the accused, he said:

'The accused spoke in Eggy and I spoke it as a teenager your honour.'

For all those Hunters kids out there who have forgotten how to speak the language of the people or you need to brush up ... enjoy the phrases detailed below. And for all those new to the language, please try the simple phrases below and overleaf. Even today, caught in the middle of Fairfield late at night they might just save your life. They might even win you a few friends.

Heggow eggare yeggou?	How are you?
Wheggats wreggong weggith yeggour pegguss?	You seem quite sad, what's up?
Eggam neggoing beggeing feggunny beggut.	I am going to be brutally honest here.
Peggiss eggoff.	Please go away.
Yeggou eggare egga neggumpty.	You are not very smart.

Yeggou eggare teggalking sheggite.	You are talking nonsense.
Teggwo's eggup eggon yeggour cheggips.	I do hope you're going to share those chips you're eating.
Yeggou heggave egga feggace eggeven egga veggulture weggoudnae peggeck.	You're not the prettiest are you?
Smeggack heggim eggin thegge pegguss.	It may be worth slapping his face.
Seggee yeggou leggater.	Catch you later on.
Teggwo heggeads eggare beggetter theggan weggon.	Two heads are better than one.
Eggits neggo eggover teggill eggits eggover.	It's not over till its over.
Eggoot eggof seggight eggoot eggof meggind.	Out of sight out of mind.
Sheggut yeggour pegguss.	Please be quiet.
Eggam seggayin neggothing teggil eggy seggee meggy leggawyer.	I would like to speak to my lawyer.
Eggam weggisnae theggere eggand yeggou cegganae preggove eggit.	I certainly wasn't there.
Reggun eggits the peggigs.	Run it's Police Scotland.
Theggy cegguffs eggare fegguckin heggurtin.	Excuse me officer but those handcuffs are a bit tight, are they not?

Eggy heggave egga creggiminal reggecored eggas leggong eggas yegger eggarm.	I have a number of past criminal convictions.
Yegga deggancer segguspended seggentence.	That went better than expected.
Sheggut yegger pegguss.	If you wouldn't mind being quiet.
Yeggou geggoing teggay theggy deggancin?	Are you going nightclubbing?
Eggy degginae keggen.	I don't know.
Eggit weggas heggoachin.	It was very busy.
Eggy eggam sceggunnered.	I am bored.
Yeggour leggooking peggeely weggalley.	You don't look very well.
Leggum.	Chimney.
Pegginkie.	Little finger.
Eggy keggen wheggat yeggou meggean.	I know what you mean.
Teggo heggaver.	To talk rubbish.
Steggop yeggour geggirning.	Stop moaning.

Photographs

2

'Wet night in Hunters', 1960s

Ruthven Avenue and Ruthven Place, 1988
Ruthven Place, 1988

Feus Hoose *(in distance)*
Hunter Crescent, 1988

Hunter Crescent, 1990

Hunter Crescent, 1990
Opposite: Early Fairfield residents, Alex and Betty McGoldrick,
get the key of the door

Alice Mcguire *(centre)*
Opposite: Jane Hall, Hunters' chippy

'At the Berries I' – Jenny Folan (Aunty Jenny)
'At the Berries II'

'Picking Tatties in Glencarse' – the author
'At the Berries III'

'Licence to pick' – Berry Bus

Alice Mcguire

CHAPTER SEVEN

Food Glorious Food

THE CHOICE OF FOOD today is unbelievable. The same goes for fast food outlets. I think in Perth, there must be over thirty takeaways. When I was young we had the Wimpy Bar in Kinnoull Street, which was hardly fast. There was another burger joint and that was in Dickson's cafe. My dad would take my brother and I there on a Sunday after mass at St John's Church. While others were praising the Lord, I was thinking about the tasty onions and cheese on my burger.

Most mums in Hunter Crescent must have worked miracles to feed their children, as back in the day money was tight and most people who were working would have been in the main on low wages. There was a staple diet of foods we would all have eaten back then. Homemade soup which could last a few days and which you would eat while filling up with plain bread.

The first sign that homemade soup was on the go was being sent over to the butchers over the Crieff Road bridge for a ham shank, a cheap piece of meat that was added to the soup. Tasty bits of meat would be scraped off it when cooked. You cannot beat the smell of your mum's homemade soup radiating through the house.

Sausage casserole, stovies, mashed tatties and cheese, corned beef hash, mince and tatties, I loved them all and can still smell them today. But the one I feared and hated was stew. I would be in tears when I knew stew was for tea as it meant two things: fat on the stew and a dry mix veg called *swell* – I hated it! And just like everyone in the Crescent there wasn't a second option. I can imagine saying to my mum:

'I'm not wanting stew, can I have stovies mum?'.

The answer to this question would have been the same in every house in Hunters:

'Like it or lump it'.

Other delicacies were fish fingers, tinned burgers, and Findus pancakes – all were served with homemade chips. It was an unwritten law that every kitchen in Hunters had a chip pan and every chip pan used cooking fat – none of that namby-pamby vegetable oil or virgin olive oil. The cooking fat oil would be used for about a week, then would be changed. The old stuff was poured down the sink; pipes were made of harder stuff back then. Our downstairs neighbour Willie Ferguson used to throw his out the kitchen window, which meant you couldn't play football in that corner of the garden as it stank and was like a skating rink.

Talking about homemade chips, the best homemade chips I ever tasted were cooked by a wee woman called Irene Burns, my pal Willie's mum. Sometimes if you were outside playing she would make you chips and put them in a paper bag for you. They lived at 16A Hunter Crescent. Any time I went to their house I was always made welcome. It always felt like their home was a busy home with Willie, his mum, his Dad Felix and a full rabble of sisters, Jackie, Christine, Kate and Fiona. I spent many a winter's Sunday night in their front bedroom listening with Willie, Christine, and Fiona to the *Top 40*. We would murder the music by joining in and trying to tape it and stop it before the DJ started speaking – back in the day that was a real skill.

The kids now are in and out of fast food restaurants morning, noon, and night. It's become the norm and must cost a fortune. When we were kids, fast food was running up the stairs to get a tomato sauce, salad cream, or sugar piece, which was bread spread with margarine or butter and sprinkled with sugar. Sometimes you were forced to sit down and have a plate of soup and a slice of bread. You were running about all day long – it was probably a struggle to make sure you were eating as many calories as you were burning up.

It's no longer a treat to go for something from a fast food outlet or chippy. A chippy treat was a big thing in my day. We would get one if my dad had just been paid for a job. As well as his day job of being a slater he was also the local chimney sweep and dentist to the kids of Hunters. (I say dentist, he wasn't doing root canal treatment or bridgework but for some reason the kids would come to the house if they had a loose baby tooth. He would put a piece of tissue round it, tell them to look up, and nine times out of ten, the tooth would fall out.)

My dad would usually go to the chippy over the road – the Chinese chippy called Good Luck Chippy. He would go all continental and order a Chicken Maryland. Mum would get a Mock Chop Supper; my brother and I would be on the chips and curry that was served in paper – it tasted better in paper than it does now in these horrible plastic containers.

Having a sweet was a big deal as well. You maybe got one on a Saturday and/or Sunday, and if that was an Arctic Roll or even a tin of fruit with a slab of vanilla ice cream it was an *Oh ya Dancer Moment*. Now, everyone is having fancy cheesecake, pavlova, and the like. And let's not forget the good old ice-cream float – a spoonful of ice cream topped up with Coca-Cola. It was no oil painting but it was a thing of beauty.

When the summer came along the good old Hunters Salad would appear. Salads now a-days are a work of art with a vast array of continental meats, green onion, red onion, avocado, celery, couscous, goats cheese, shredded lettuce, shredded carrot, glazed walnuts, and feta – the list is endless. The Hunters Salad was slightly different. It was lettuce leaves, halved tomatoes, spam, chopped pork, ham, garlic sausage, chopped cucumber, a hard-boiled egg, plain crisps, and salad cream – not even mayonnaise.

I remember someone in the Crescent promising us all a cold fizzy drink from a Soda Stream, which was all the craze in the 1970s. I could not wait to get my chops around a glass of this stuff as I had seen the advert on television for months. Disappointment doesn't quite cover it. I was offered a host of tropical flavours. Every one of them tasted the same: bland, fizzy, tonic water.

One thing we had that was better was the choice of sweets and chocolates and they tasted better. Every shop had a penny sweet section. You would go into Scott's with your 10p and start picking your way through the penny sweets, which were stored in a tray of small compartments called the penny-mix tray, while Enid with her hawk eyes watched you weren't trying any hand tricks to sneak in a Penny Bubbly. You would repeatedly pick up something and ask how much:

'One pence',

you would get in a stern voice.

'How much?'

'Two pence'

would be the reply.

By this time the voice had a pissed off tone about it.

The choice was endless and it was never an easy decision. Fruit Salads, Penny Dainties, Black Jacks, Refreshers, Sherbet Fountains, Chocolate Tools, Chocolate Ice Cups, Bubblies, Foam Bananas and Shrimps, Flying Saucers, and Lucky Tatties – I could go on and on but I'm salivating all over the laptop keys.

Now if you were flush (you had for example found 50p on the street) chocolate was within your budget. Again the choice was endless. This is sad but I can remember my first Yorkie Bar. For months, I had watched this advert with some big hard man truck driver eating a Yorkie – a brick of solid chocolate. It was out of my price range at 15p but somehow I wangled 50p from my mum, went sauntering into Scott's and asked for a Yorkie Bar and a Gold Cup for my wee pal Willie. Think Jimmy the shopkeeper was taken aback and kept his hands on the two bars of chocolate till he saw the *Colour of my Money*.

Crisps were another thing I think were better when we were young. Scott's or the chippy would have boxes and boxes of Smith's and Golden Wonder crisps with a hole punched in the boxes for easy access. You know what put me off crisps. Think I was about ten when I bought a packet of Oxo flavoured Golden Wonder crisps from Todd's. About an hour later I thought I was having a stroke. Apparently it was just heartburn.

As the year wore on plans for orchard raiding would be afoot. One of the first times I did this was with Eddie Frampton and it was not for apples or pears. We planned to steal rhubarb from a garden in Stanley Crescent, just a short trip over the white bridge. Frampton was like the Alan Sugar of Hunter Crescent – he had planned to sell the rhubarb around the doors for a tidy profit (60:40 in his favour).

After we hopped over the fence and started helping ourselves, pulling as much of the rhubarb out the ground as we could and loading it into black bags, the kitchen door swung open and this old guy with a massive belly came flying out thrashing a bamboo cane – cracking it like a circus ringmaster and bellowing:

'Fuck off ya scavengers!'

as we leapt the fence with a handful of rhubarb each.

I remember taking some home and dipping it in sugar, it was rank rotten. Don't think I have eaten it since.

Apple and plum orchards are a plenty in Perth. There was a large back garden in Balhousie Street behind the wall that backed onto the car park of Perth City Boys Club. Willie Burns, two brothers from Muirton, Jimmy and Graham Ayton, who played for the Perth City Boys Club football team, and I organised a raid on it.

I think Jimmy was an over-age player. He was too old to play for us but we would have given him a new birth date to make him a year younger. Jimmy was small in stature but a powerful player – a general in the middle of the pitch. He was also the general when it came to planning the raid on the apple orchard in Balhousie Street. The plan required Jimmy, Willie, and Graham to climb the wall and raid the place while I stood and guarded the bikes – like a sort of low budget getaway driver.

Early at football training Graham was at the wind up and called Willie and me *'a couple of Hunters minks'*. I'm sure we replied with an equally derogatory remark. During the raid I seized the chance to get him back by loosening all the bolts on his bike. So after ten minutes into the fruit heist the three raiders came running out of the dark by the side of the house hollering:

'Run ... the old bastard's coming after us!'.

We all jumped on our bikes and started peddling up Balhousie Street when we heard the old guy shouting and getting into his car and speeding after us. It was at this stage, Graham's bike started to come apart. He had no control over where he was going and I'm sure he was eventually left only with a pair of handle bars – the rest of the bike spread all over the road – before shouting:

'Camilleri yer a bastard!'.

I think the old guy took pity on him and helped him pick up the parts of his bike he had left behind him.

All this raiding was useless as the fruit was always sour. Cakes on the other hand were always edible and there was a bakery nearby on Feus Road. I think it was McIntyre's. Willie and I had a set routine that worked every time. We would go along to the old redbrick building in the evening and Willie would go to the side door – where I recall there was a counter – and in his deepest 14-year old voice ask:

'Are yer rolls ready mate?'.

The poor baker would have to go and check in the warehouse while I'd swoop in and grab a couple of domino cakes, which you don't get now (they were big rectangular sponge cakes covered in chocolate icing and decorated like a domino).

Cakes like fast food were a luxury then. So were biscuits. As I said earlier my mum worked miracles with the money she had to work with. She would always manage to throw a couple of packets of biscuits in the shopping – none of those fancy chocolate digestives, Kit Kats, or Jacob's Clubs though. I think she always picked biscuits she liked: Pink Wafers, Rich Tea, and Garibaldi – I hated them all but this may have been a wise tactic because we usually still had biscuits left by Thursday.

On top of this my mum would sometimes bake scones or a fruit cake. Then my dad started getting in on the act thinking he was a baker. Unfortunately his cakes were so heavy he needed to get a couple of neighbours to help him lift them out of the oven and then borrow a chainsaw to slice them. To use an old Scottish word, they were *boggin*.

There were great foods and not so great foods the people of Hunter Crescent got by on. I ate some fantastic meals and some foods that I will never eat again. One thing you could not say about kids from Hunter Crescent and that is they were underfed. We all ate well and fortunately we didn't need charity or food banks.

CHAPTER EIGHT

Fun and Games

I COULD BE WRONG but I am sure children are born with a USB port. They come home from school and plug themselves into all the latest technology. It's a very different world now. The choice of entertainment is endless: laptops, internet, PlayStation 4s, Xbox Ones, iPads, and more. As for mobile phones, we didn't take selfies with the phone we had, ours was at the end of the Crescent and you needed coins to use it. Just to add to the ambient feeling of the phone box it would be vandalised, stinking of pee, or burnt out. Instead of a USB port we had an imagination – and you never ran out of storage.

You would go out in the morning and be outside all day playing, maybe going back for dinner – then your tea. You could not be contacted but we knew when it was time to get home. Most of my youth in Hunter Crescent was spent playing football with my brother John and friends Willie Burns, Mark Costello, Steve Ferguson, Fareed Tanyous, Jason Furlong, and Eddie Frampton. To me, these names are a classic line-up that could have won a *Housing Scheme World Cup* against Muirton, Letham, North Muirton, Tulloch, and Hillyland.

Our home pitch was a surface I have never seen or played on anywhere else. Our *Field of Dreams* was a base of tarmac covered with broken glass of every colour imaginable. Even the infamous *Ten Green Bottles Sitting on a Wall* ended up on our pitch – it was a death trap. Instead of blades of grass we had shards of glass. In sunlight it looked like millions of diamonds shining but if you fell or slipped it was like falling into a school of piranha fish. You had to be brave or an utter idiot to play any kind of sport on it. And as I'll explain, the squad we had possessed both characteristics.

My brother John was your standard hard man midfielder. He was quite happy to put you six feet in the air and onto the concrete and glass. How *hard* was he you ask? He would sometimes wear an

England football shirt when we played, so you work it out. Willie was an old style player. He was one of those now extinct breed of skilful players who could turn on a ha'penny. As few people dropped that much money in Hunters, there was no opportunity to actually prove it.

Mark Costello was a good steady player, the kind that would get the job done but get cut from the highlights on *Match of the Day*. Steven Ferguson was a good player considering his footwear varied from steel-toe cap boots to winkle pickers. Fareed Tanyous could be a tricky player but a bit lazy. He had the talent but he couldn't tackle a fish supper or come to think of it a white pudding. Jason Furlong was a good wee player as well who could run further than his name suggested.

Eddie was the King of the Taepunt (toe punt) and when he hit the sweet spot the ball would burst the net. I say net but it was actually a chainlink fence. I was, and always will be, a goalkeeper but on that surface I played outfield – I had my looks to think about. There were other players but we were the heart of the squad.

We would play for hours: *First to Twenty* (usually 2 versus 2 or 3 versus 3 and changed ends when one team got to ten); *World Cup* (one goalkeeper with anything from three to twenty-five players – once you scored you were through to the next round of the game which would go on until only two were left. Often when one of the final two scored a face was punched because of arguments over deflections and who's goal it was); and *Wally* (a game for two to two hundred players who had to kick a ball off a wall – if you missed the wall you were out. The game would go on until only one player was left). This game was the cause of more broken windows than any other and when you heard the glass shatter we were like a gang of meerkats running for cover in every direction. Once the victim came out and stabbed our ball with a pair of scissors before gutting it like a chicken – we knew the game was a *Bogey*.

Another place we would sometimes play football was the firing range of Perth Gun Club, round the back of Jeanfield Swifts' at Simpson Park. To get there, you crossed the White Bridge, an iconic landmark of Hunter Crescent. Built in the mid-1950s, it must have been a boon for people wanting to travel from Muirton to Hunter

Crescent and vice versa, as before it was constructed you would have to go over the Crieff Road, which was an extra fifteen minutes travelling time.

By the 1970s and 1980s, the White Bridge was a no-go area after dark. If you were returning home from a friend's at night and you headed towards the bridge, if there was a menacing figure standing at the top of the bridge with the odd orange glow from the fag he was smoking you would take the long option. Even during the day there would be the odd brawl, especially after school. Perth Grammar and St Columba pupils would clash over shouts of *'Fenian bastards'* or *'Proddie bastards'* ... my pal Willie and I used to just walk past it all, religion and race were never an issue with Hunters bairns.

The first rule of gun club was to play there when the members were not practising. The range was a grass pitch like a bowling green. It was used for international games against our rivals Muirton. Many say the oldest football international in the world is Hunters versus Muirton. These matches were all very cordial to begin with like the game on the Somme on Christmas Day. Shaking of hands and calls of *'Well played'* would usually be the order of the day but sometimes there would be allegations of cheating and as we headed back over the White Bridge, or as we called it *Checkpoint Charlie*, the abuse would begin.

They would start with *'Tinky bastards'* and we would retort with *'Yer shite'*. Football rivalries are like that, cruel with lots of nasty and hurtful name calling. The greatest game we ever played in was against Hillyland: 6-1 down at half-time, we managed to turn it around to 7-6. The fact that our striker threatened to punch their goalkeeper in the puss every time he was through on goal had nothing to do with it.

Occasionally we went up market and played in Mrs White's back green that was like Hampden Park. We even had washing poles as goalposts. The only downside was the ten-foot fence, topped with spikes, that separated the green from the railway line – it was like a cemetery for footballs that fence. A match would start and Mrs White's bedroom window would open:

'Away fae here now'.

I would try to reassure her no windows would be broken but all I would get is:

'*Moooooooove, ma man's on the nightshift'*.

My proudest moment in football has to be playing for Hunters Rangers when I was twelve against much older guys. I was also the first Catholic to play for them after a boy from Muirton didn't turn up so they were one short. I was told not to say I was a Catholic but I think my name gave it away. These games were played on the park of broken glass to big crowds and a selection of Irish rebel music blasting out from one bedroom window and the *Sash* from a half-open window on the other side. There was no trouble but it was genuinely an incredible atmosphere to play in.

Other friends that I had back then that were not part of the football *Illuminati* included Robert Cummins who was more into his clothes, music, and bikes, and Jackie Legg. Jackie was no footballer – he was just into pure mischief, from dropping fireworks through letterboxes to putting worms down your back.

Occasionally we would get bored of football, which was rare, and would play other games: *British Bulldog, Kick the Can*, and *Kiss, Cuddle, and Torture* – I would usually ask for all three if Tracy McCullie caught me but usually I got a slap in the chops. *Kerby* was a very popular game. You had to rebound a ball off the kerb and if you caught it you went into the middle for a bonus. All these games were played by boys and girls.

Girls also had their own games such as *Beddies*. This usually involved getting one of your mum's ornaments and smashing it so you had chalk to mark out your *Beddies*. The marker was usually an old tin with stones in it. *Shoppies* was another game which boys would get roped into. It required old bottles and tins for stock, grass and leaves to sell as salad – the currency was usually stones.

Girls would play skipping for hours either with individual skipping-ropes or a longer rope operated by two while one was in the middle. Occasionally there would be two ropes and it would take Olympic-grade skipping not to get lassoed by the ropes. Songs would be added to the skill. These included:

Skinny Malinky Longlegs

Skinny Malinky Longlegs
Big banana feet
Went to the pictures
Couldnae find a seat
When the picture started
Skinny Malinky farted
Skinny Malinky Longlegs
Big banana feet

Eeeny Meeny Miney Mo

Eeeny meeny miney mo
Put the baby on the po
When he's done
Wipe his bum
And tell his mum what he's done

You Cannae Shove yer Granny off the Bus

You cannae shove yer granny off the bus
You cannae shove yer granny off the bus
You cannae shove yer granny
Because she's yer mammy's mammy
You cannae shove yer granny off the bus

Another great spectator sport was rounders. On a nice evening neighbours would hang out the window, sit in the close doorway and watch the action. Two teams would be picked – worst players usually left till last – one fielding, one batting. I say bat but it could be a tennis racket or an old leg of a table. The game could be played for a few hours and it was a lot of fun – it would bring neighbours together.

There was a great wee swing park behind 7-9 Hunter Crescent.

It was the *Jewel in the Crown* with two sets of old wooden swings and a roundabout that holds a sad memory for me. On 26 July 1974, while pushing my cousin Steven Park on the roundabout, he fell off cutting his hand and needed to go to the PRI for stitches ... later that afternoon my granny died.

It was great when the council cut the grass at this wee park. We would pile the cuttings up into a mountain of fresh grass then get really high on the swings and dive off – hours of fun but not for my brother who would be eaten alive by the fleas and be covered in fleabites. You would get the odd kid landing on his head from about ten feet in the air. They would get up, then there would usually be five-seconds of silence before the greetin' would start. Nowadays the council would be looking at lawsuits – back then it was part of growing up.

John and Fareed used to go about on their bikes like the two American TV cops in *Chips*. I think they both had Grifter bikes, the *it* bike of the time. (I think Eddie Frampton was their boss as he had a sought after Raleigh Chopper bike.) They used to cruise round Hunters patrolling the streets looking for trouble. God knows why, as neither could fight sleep. The team disbanded after going round the side of a block of flats into a back green and Fareed nearly having his head taken clean off by a washing rope. It's a shame, I would love to see them get back together and get back on the Grifters before they are fifty.

Sometimes we would build a pair of ramps in the middle of the road and that's when injuries were ten a penny. Evil Knievel was all the rage at that time. We didn't have any buses to jump over, so we took turns lying between the ramps. I had a crap fold-up bike – no gears nor brakes – but still decided to try a jump over Eddie Frampton, my brother John, and Willie Burns. Pedalling like a man possessed, I managed to clear them but because I had no suspension, as I touched the other side my bike collapsed like a stack of cards leaving me with grazed knees and a black eye.

If you ever had an issue with a bike there was only one guy to go and see ... you've heard of the *Horse Whisperer*, we had the *Bike Whisperer*: Michael Morison, also known as Moses, son of a lovely wee woman, Peggy, and the greatest berry bus driver in the West,

Eck Morison. Moses built his own bikes and could fix most problems on a bike. He's the guy you would see going down the road full pelt doing a wheelie, folded arms, fag in his mouth – top guy.

Bobby Summers who lived at 7 Hunter Crescent was another guy who was brilliant at making things. In fact I was his crash-test dummy until enough was enough. He had built a bogie kart, which we took to the top of the brae on the Crieff Road facing the new nursery – no breaks, no steering wheel, just a set of reins made from rope and the seat was a piece of wood. As we stood at the top and I got into the bogie his last concerned words were:

'Dinnae break it'.

Halfway down and at full speed, I hit a rabbit hole and went about six feet in the air and started rolling down the hill through jaggy nettles, landing winded at the bottom. This was just the beginning. As I looked up the bogie looked like it was bouncing in slow motion down the hill before it landed on top of me accompanied by the distant sound of Bobby's evil laugh. I was in tears; bruised ribs and a cut lip tends to do that to you. On that day, I told Formula 1 to *'F'k off'*.

Bobby was a hunting, shooting, and fishing kind of guy. I actually went fishing with him a few times. He knew loads of stuff about wildlife and always seemed more worldly wise than the rest of us. One summer there was a bit of a rat infestation coming from the railway tracks at the back of our house. Bobby came up to the house and went up to our first-floor flat bedroom window. He had this big metal catapult and, using ball-bearings, he took out the rats, like Hunters' very own Robin Hood – like he was at a funfair shooting gallery. There was one ball-bearing that ricocheted off a washing pole and went through Stan Hughes's kitchen window but we'll not mention that!

The most dangerous thing I probably did was bee-keeping. All you needed to set up your bee business was an old TC lemonade bottle and some flowers at the bottom to feed your stock. It took great skill to catch bees and wasps, and only the proper tough would catch hornets. You would try to coax them in telepathically, opening the lid so they could see the tasty flowers in the bottom of the bottle. Once you lured one in, you would close the lid quickly. After a few hours of collecting, you had a vibrating glass bottle. I would show remorse and throw the bottle on to the railway line. As it smashed, the bees, wasps, and hornets achieved their freedom.

Hunters kids could strip a car very quickly. The Crescent was a haven for dumped cars. For whatever reason – the usual one being that someone from Hunter Crescent had *borrowed* a car from somewhere else in Perth – a car would be dumped in the car park behind 25 Hunter Crescent (in the shadow of the White Bridge). Like a troop of chimps, we would approach the Ford Cortina (or such like), then one by one we would explore the car, opening the bonnet, pulling out spark plugs and wires, while somebody pretended to drive the car. One or two of the other chimps would jump up and down on the roof or slide down the windscreen onto the bonnet. Hours of fun was had until one of the troop got their fingers slammed in a door or a piece of glass lodged in their eye after someone decided to lob the car battery thought the windscreen.

Another place we would hang out was the White Building, which was an old railway goods yard. I use the word building loosely as it had been knocked to the ground and was now a mass area of what looked like a war zone with piles of bricks and rubble everywhere. The only thing intact was the loading bay, underneath which were all sorts of rat runs and cubbyholes we would go through. It was pitch black and you could easily disappear, never to be seen again. It was littered with beer cans and wine and spirit bottles, all empty I may add. There were also Mother's Pride bread bags everywhere – you would be forgiven for thinking people were having underground picnics, sadly not. In the late seventies into the eighties, glue-sniffing had become an epidemic, especially on a rundown housing estate like Hunter Crescent.

Young kids and teenagers would steal glue from schools (EVO-STIK glue from woodwork classes mainly) or somehow buy it and disappear up a rundown close or a derelict building in a small group, They would put some of the glue into the plastic Mother's Pride bag and inhale it … not sniff it. The term glue-inhaler isn't as catchy as glue-sniffer. As I said, glue-sniffing was rife at the time and even a few of my friends tried it. Glue-sniffers would just appear out of nowhere in a zombie state, eyes glazed over, with lost demeanour – they just seemed to float into view. They would just walk through the middle of a game of football in the park as if they were the only people in the park. In fact one former glue-sniffer told me he and his mates were high on glue one time when they decided all the broken glass in the park looked like diamonds. They were actually so convinced they started picking bits of glass up and putting them in their pockets, thinking they were onto a money-spinner.

Some glue-sniffers moved on to sniffing gas and lighter fuel. All were on a one way ticket to planet Zoom (high on glue) but never seemed to realise it was a long way back to planet Earth. When the buzz ran out they would tend to look confused and not quite sure where they had been. They were never violent nor aggressive. In fact, if anything, they looked like lost souls, not sure where they were or who they were.

Drinking was another pastime some of the older lads were into. You would see them sitting in the long grass up at the *Dump* or under the White Bridge necking such delights as half-bottles of whisky and cheap cider. I imagine these were the aperitifs before the downing of cans of McEwan's Export, Harp Lager, and every red-blooded young man's favourite, Tennent's Lager which featured a scantily clad women called Marie, Erica, or May … ding-dong.

In the winter we would still be outside playing football. When Willie and I signed for our first team, Perth City Boys Club under-14s, we began training at the old PCBC building, which was an old wooden building on the Dunkeld Road – now long gone. The team was generally made up of boys from Hunters and Muirton. We spent many a happy Thursday night training there and played games on a Sunday visiting football hotbeds like Dunkeld, Kinross, and Almondbank.

We were actually not a bad team, even running Letham to a 1-1 draw. Letham was a team that would generally beat teams by rugby scores but you just learned to except defeat unlike today where everyone's a winner and everybody gets a badge – but they do not learn how to handle disappointment and defeat.

When we stayed inside we would pass the time playing Subbuteo, a tabletop football game that was all the craze when we were young – it was hours of fun, flicking players round a green baize. We would organise games that were better run than FIFA. Most of the gang had their grounds except Steven Ferguson. He would play his games in the close, which was a nightmare if people were going in and out – the fear of your star striker being stood on or run over by a pram was very real. My favourite ground was Eddie Frampton's. It was a tight ground and when taking a corner you had to crawl under the bed to flick your player but it was the catering I liked. Eddie's mum, Izzy, used to do the best curries in Perth … no question. She would put her head round the door and say:

'*Ye want some curry son?*'.

She would later return with a giant plate of rice and curry – better than pie and Bovril any day.

Outwith the Crescent, Willie and I would go and watch our local team, Jeanfield Swifts. We could watch the games from my bedroom window but we couldn't see the faraway goal. We would crawl under the railway fence and run across two sets of rail tracks rather than go over the Crieff Road or White Bridge, We would also go to watch St Johnstone at Muirton Park, hanging about the turnstiles, asking for a lift over. I can remember Eddie Frampton having a wee scam going selling St Johnstone prize draw tickets or it could have been programmes and bagging the money then going back a few weeks later pretending to be someone else – always the entrepreneur.

The *Tin Hut* (its official title was the Smith-Lockart Centre) holds a very special place in most people's hearts from my generation of Hunters folk. It was brought to Hunters in a lorry from the back of a warehouse in the Feus Road. Jake Sinclair and others constructed it with the hope that the youth of Hunters would have somewhere do go when they had nothing to do.

It's the discos that people remember: Rocky's Super Sounds with

Rab Sinclair on the decks as *'Town called Malice'* was blasting out. Rab would give it a *'one two, one two'*, just to make sure everything was in order. I didn't go a lot but when I did it was always well run with Mr Sinclair sitting outside the door taking the money. You got the back of your hand stamped. I recall that you would get people who wouldn't wash the back of their hand all week so they could get in free the following week. When you went into the dance area, boys were on one side, girls on the other.

There was a wee tuck shop – I used to get discount if Cathrine Sinclair was there. This was a parent no-go zone but occasionally a mum, sometimes a dad, would turn up looking for their son or daughter. At this stage, they would be hiding and the rest of us would deny ever seeing them there.

Another great source of entertainment was messing about on the water. We didn't have a posh boat like a punt, we had the blown up inner tube of a lorry or tractor tyre, which would magically appear if 'the sun was splitting the trees'. Our choice of water was the Lade that snaked up the back of Hunters along the back of Simpson Park and into town. We would spend hours floating up and down the Lade on these low-budget dingys throwing stones at the ducks and the odd water rat while at the same time trying to avoid old prams, bikes, beer cans, and wine bottles. You could only go as far as the arch at the Crieff Road bridge.

I recall an incident where someone had driven over the side of the road leading out of Simpson Park, their motor going down the steep verge into the Lade. It was there for weeks. A gang of us thought it would be a good idea for us to see if we could get into it – cannot remember the task force in total but do remember the operation going wrong and resident danger man Robert Hughes finding a way in through the boot but found himself trapped and some do-gooder phoning emergency services and with the sound of sirens we bolted and left him to it. Next day the car was pulled from the Lade and our sunken treasure with it.

Adults from Hunters would frequent the pub called the *Feus Hoose* locally known as the *Feusy*. It seemed to have a bit of a reputation as being a bit of a rough house, so rough in fact rumour has it even the pool table had bandages on its legs. All the old wine and beer specialists, however, tell me it was a great pub with a great atmosphere. Back in the day, the darts, pool, and domino teams at the *Feusy* were some of the best in Perthshire.

Another place and much trendier was the *Yorkie*. At that time, there were a lot of African and Arab flight students studying at Scone Aerodrome. A number of girls from Hunters dated these guys. Sometimes when you saw five sharp dressed black guys walking into Hunters, you could mistake them for the popular group of the 1970s, the *Commodores,* or think you were watching a scene from a *Shaft* movie. The girls would get a hard time for dating these guys. As they walked through Hunters with their sharp dressed dates, people would shout out the window:

'*Darkie lover!*'.

Some neighbours would say:

'*I see such and such is a darkie lover, she's going with a boy from the aerodrome*'.

All recognised as totally unacceptable behaviour today.

Sometimes on a Friday or Saturday night you could hear some of the old boys heading back into Hunters from way over the Crieff Road bridge, getting louder as they got closer. The best singer of them all was Jocky White, he would be singing a Frank Sinatra or Dean Martin number and he was as good as them. If there was such a thing as *Hunter Crescent X Factor*, Jocky would win it.

Hunters was famous for its house parties. They could go on for days, with dozens of people crammed into Hunters homes, especially at New Year. The kitchen table acting as a bar would be stacked with tins of beer, bottles of spirits, and old savoury favourites: nibbles like crisps, sausage rolls, and peanuts. I think I took a sneaky swig of Bacardi at one of these parties aged about twelve – it put me off drink for life.

The Silver Jubilee was living proof of how Hunter Crescent could organise a party. For me this is one of my greatest memories of my sixteen years in the Crescent. Neighbours clubbed together to make sandwiches, cakes, sausage rolls, and tablet, laying them out on rows of tables; loads of games were organised as well. It was so well coordinated. Even the vandals were patriotic in 1977. They sprayed on a side of a wall *God save the Queen*; and again when Charles and Diana got married, it was a big event in Hunter Crescent.

CB radio (Citizen's Band radio) was all the rage in the early 1980s and Hunter Crescent had its fair share of users, all with their own *Handle* (nickname): Disco Kid, Lady Lux, Rob Roy, Gando, and Fraulein, to name a few. The other Perth housing schemes also had their own handles. Some that spring to mind include: Beverly Hills (Letham), Hollywood (Hillyland), Old Rio Grande (Muirton), New Rio Grande (North Muirton), Alabama (Potterhill), Salt Lake City (Craigie), Shaky Town (Hunter Crescent). The best of them all was Little Africa (Scone), a name given because of the students from the Middle East and Africa who were studying at Scone Aerodrome.

People would talk on CB and even arrange to *eyeball*, meaning to meet up. One of my friends had a rig and we would sit talking on it late at night to all sorts. Over a few nights I got speaking to a girl from Old Rio Grande who sounded lovely and after about two weeks of talking we decided to meet on the White Bridge. As I climbed the steps of the bridge I began to realise she was not as good looking as she sounded and looked like the love child of Dot Cotton and Sid James. As I approached her she asked me if I was Apollo Creed. I nervously said no and scampered over the bridge implementing Plan B, a white pudding supper from the Good Luck Chinese chippy on the Dunkeld Road.

Photographs

3

The Tin Hut
'The Wall of Dignity' *(Perthshire Advertiser)*

Rab Sinclair, The Tin Hut in-house DJ
Inside The Tin Hut *(Perthshire Advertiser)*

'The Transit' – Hunters' transport of choice, 1988
'Hunters day out' – 11 Hunter Crescent in background where the author grew up
Opposite: Hearn's Post Office & Grocery, 1980s

'Happy in Hunters', 1988
The Shooting Range

Hunters Village, a new team in the Perthshire
amateur ranks *(Perthshire Advertiser)*
'Street party', 1980s

Feus Hoose ladies' darts team *(Perthshire Advertiser)*

White Bridge and Lade
White Bridge *(photograph: Fiona McWilliams)*

Hunter Crescent, c1990
Previous: By the Community House

Bread van outside Tollhoose Stores
Tollhoose Stores

Boy with Hunters' Snowman

Bonfire burn marks on wall, Hunter Crescent c1990
This page and opposite: Demolition work, Hunter Crescent, c1990
(Photographs: John Lloyd)

Play park behind 7/9 Hunter Crescent

Hunter Crescent kids *(photograph: James A. F. Herd)*

CHAPTER NINE

Memories

'We lived in Ruthven Avenue before moving to 11F Hunter Crescent around 1977. We lived in a great close with good neighbours and a great sense of community. I remember in the winter months we used to have snooker competitions on a small table in the living room with Fred and his two sons.' — *Angie Brown*

'It could be a bit rough and ready when I lived there in the 1960s: people worked hard and played hard. It was never quiet. I can remember a massive street fight with stones being thrown from one end of the Crescent to the other – mainly just young kids. The Salvation Army used to come round on a Sunday trying to save all our souls – mission impossible! They would turn up with the brass band blasting out 'Onward Christian Soldiers'. It was a lively place in the 1960s with a never-ending noise of so many people living in one area. You would hear housewives arguing about who wasn't taking their turn to clean the communal close, more than anything else. Actually, there was a garden that used to compete for the best garden in Perth and he had a model of the Smeaton's Perth Bridge in it. It could be a bit rough and ready but there was a lot of decent people who looked out for each other. I have a lot of happy memories of my time growing up there.'   — *Jim Cameron*

'I had a lot of family in Hunter Crescent and grew up there as well – so many great memories. It was a lovely place to live in the 1950s and 1960s. I made so many friends I am still in touch with. When the council started ripping out all the gardens that's when it all started to go downhill – a real shame.'
                    — *Rachel Camilleri (née Park)*

'I left when I was about seven. I can still remember a number of my neighbours: Willie Ferguson and Helen Blair next door. I can also remember that when the trains used to pass the back of the house the house used to shake.Our back garden was like a jungle – the grass was about five feet high! I can also remember all the different vans that used to come round including the ragman. So many silly memories: I can always remember going to Scott's for curry crisps! And I can also remember throwing Tonka trucks out John Camilleri's bedroom window at my big brother William. Thank God we missed or it would have killed him, ha-ha-ha. As I said I was very young when I left but have only happy memories of the place.'

— Karl Conterio

'In Hunter Crescent we had great times spending the summer at the berry picking. We could spend hours doing something so simple like skipping with a large skipping rope with all the kids joining in. We used to meet up with friends at the swings at the end of the street and play what seemed like endless summer days.' **— Catherine Dixon**

'Growing up in Hunters was an adventure! Building gang huts from stuff we found in skips. Getting tick under your mother's name. Hiding when the Provy man was at the door, going to the berries. Never get that kind of community nowadays. Best years of my life.' **— Robert Cullen Duff**

'Growing up in Hunter Crescent in the 1970s and 1980s was a fantastic time for me. Everyone looked out for each other and I made so many friends that I am still in contact with today. So many funny stories that involve John Camilleri, John Young, and Alex Williamson. One involved the three of us going down to the bakery down the Feus Road. We would hide until they started putting the rolls outside to cool. When the time was right, we would grab trays of rolls and run like Mo Farrah while being chased by a couple of bakers until we reached the sanctuary of the Crescent; that's when we knew we were safe. We would then sell them round the doors. I remember a guy who liked a drink on a Sunday night called Mexican Andy. He would turn into the Hulk picking up full metal buckets of rubbish and throwing them up in the air! I also remember big games of football in the park between Dunc Macdonald's Hunters Rangers versus Paddy McCole's Hunters Celtic – they even wore the club colours. I think Tony Camilleri was the first Catholic to play for Hunters Rangers. There were always big crowds watching the games, you even had someone blasting out Orange Lodge songs on a big speaker through an open bedroom window.'

— ***Eddie Frampton***

'It was a great place to grow up. I was brought up at 25 Hunter Crescent. I had loads of friends. During the summer, you would be outside all day. One of my happiest memories was during the Royal Wedding of Charles and Diana, there was a big street party with loads of street games … best days of my life.'

— ***Amanda Ghekis***

'I grew up in Hunter Crescent between 1970 and 1981 – used to go about in a gang. We would collect wood for bonfires, sometimes stealing firewood from other gangs so ours was the biggest – all harmless fun. It was a hard life, the houses were very cold during the winter. I spent many a happy summer grubbing at the berries. So many happy days – great place to spend my youth.'

— ***George Gibson***

'We lived at 9 Hunter Crescent. One crazy memory of my childhood was that all the kids back then had penknives and me and my older brother James would play out the back garden a game called Knife, where you stand opposite each other and in turn you throw the penknife and where it landed you had to stretch to reach it with your foot. There was one time when I threw it and it went into my brothers toe. I had to pull it out but it never stopped us playing the game over and over again. Children in Hunters were allowed out to play at night but the minute the street lights came on, you had to go in your house – there were no ifs nor buts in those days. I used to always go to the shop for our neighbour Ina Robertson for ten Woodbine or Capstan and I was allowed to get a penny chew or a Lucky Tattie for myself – happy times.' — **Helen Gillies (née Garvie)**

'I lived at 11F Tulloch Road, which was classed as Hunters. So many good times with friends and family, great community spirit, and characters – very happy time of my life.'

— **Susan Hoolachan**

'I hated being stigmatised because of where I lived. I was so embarrassed to admit I was from Hunter Crescent when I was a teenager. I spent hours with my best friend Nicola Donaldson – we are still best friends today. Saturday night was always entertaining when all the drunks were getting thrown out The Feusy (Feus Hoose pub) – there were street fights every weekend. My happy memories are too many to mention but one that sticks out to this very day is the Queen's Silver Jubilee celebration in 1977. Hunters had loads of street parties that day; it was a beautiful summer's day. My mum and dad, Nicky and Kitty Mclean, baked and made sandwiches, cakes, and trifles, like many other families – the preparation took days. I also remember the rows and rows of tables and chairs, it just showed the community spirit of Hunter Crescent. All the press was there that day taking photos.'

— **Gaynor Hunter (née McLean)**

'I was born in 1938 at 20E Hunter Crescent. There were a lot of large families, no one had any money, and it was a bit rough – even the mice went about in pairs! A lot of good memories.'

— **Ian Imrie**

'I was born in 27B Ruthven Avenue and went around with Gaynor McLean, Shona McLeod, Erica Williamson, Carrie McPhee, and Jay Myles. We were known as the A-Team, ha-ha. We got up to harmless mischief: stealing rhubarb and then stealing my mum's sugar bowl to dip it in! Very happy times.'

— *Mandy Kerr (née Furlong)*

'I actually miss old Hunter Crescent. I lived there from 1966 till 1985 – brain not what it use to be but I always remember never really being in the house always out playing and only going home for tea or when the street lights would come on. I would play football for hours up at the park. Our family would spend the summer at the berries and the autumn at the tatties. It had a reputation for being a rough housing scheme but I have many good memories of many of the people who lived there.'

— *Kenny Leaver*

'I stayed at 18C Ruthven Avenue till 1976. I had a great childhood growing up in Hunter Crescent; great times with Dave Hool, the Smarts, and James Douglas – all best of mates when we were young lads.'

— *Brian Little*

'I was born in Ruthven Place in 1952. I can still name every one of the thirty families that lived in the cul-de-sac and in all my years I have never encountered such a strong community feeling anywhere else. As a kid, I would always have a job, from selling Sunday papers outside Todd's on a Sunday, working on Frank Morrow's grocers van, which was an old bus. And like every other Hunters kid, I picked tatties and berries. A popular meeting place was the Ten Talls where we would build our own swings. Hunters was full of real characters: hard men and even harder women. We sometimes had nothing and we didn't realise how poor we were. Hunter Crescent has produced so many amazing people, some have gone on to enhance the lives of others in Perth and I for one will always be proud of being a boy from Hunters.' — *Eddie McErlain*

'It was a great place to live in the 1950s and 1960s. By the 1970s, it was going downhill and by the early 1980s, they were setting the houses on fire and people were taking drugs in the empty closes – it was time to make a change. A lot of great people have been brought up in the Crescent. So many great memories and people.'   — *Alice Mcguire, MBE*

'We lived at 30C Hunter Crescent – loved how everyone who lived there at the time got on with each other. You could leave your doors unlocked back then, not that there was much to steal back then. The houses were also freezing back then – we used to get ice on the inside of the bedroom windows.'
                    —*Gilbert McPhee*

'I lived there from 1948 till 1967 at 29B Hunter Crescent. So many happy memories with my family back then. For some reason I always think of Easter when all the neighbours would pack picnics and go up the River Almond. It was a great place to be brought up and I had lots of friends and family.'
                    — *Sally McPherson (née McCormack)*

'I lived at 7D Tulloch Road. I just have good memories of my time there, the Hunters disco in the Tin Hut, think on a Saturday night; and so many fun times in the summers at the berries. Made so many friends back then who I'm still in touch with.'
                    — *Leigh Mearns*

'I was born at 19E Ruthven Avenue in 1946, which was my gran and grandad's house. I was one of three; my two older brothers were both born there, then we moved when I was about three to Paul Street in the Town. Then when I was five we went back to live at number 30D Ruthven Avenue. We thought it was great having our own bedrooms. They were really well built homes. I grew up there till I was 15 then the family moved to Sydney, Australia but growing up there really was fun. Really no down side – all the neighbours were family people and they all got on with living their lives. Always plenty kids to play in the street with and we had the field as we called it, bonfires, football for the young lads, and gambling on a Sunday afternoon for the older lads. When I came back from Australia I was 19 met my now hubby who lived at 23 Ruthven Avenue got married had our wedding in Feus Hoose which was lovely then. By this time my parents were living in Letham but the Avenue was full of characters. After we left for Australia my hubby and I came to Perth in 1971 with our daughter who was only eighteen months but by then the Avenue had started to really go down the tube which was really sad but those days as kids were best days of my life.'   — *Maria Meiklem (née Byczkowska)*

'I can remember spending most of my youth at the Ten Talls (although there were only nine!) and getting up to no good, like sneaking into the Bon Accord warehouse and helping ourselves to bottles of lemonade. The discos in the Tin Hut were great fun. We also used to raid Morris Young's orchard. I also remember trading my mum's brand new leather jacket my dad had just bought her with the rag and bone man for a balloon and my mum then running down the street trying to get it back. It had its problems but I have happy memories of the old place.'
    — *Mandy Millar (née McQuaid)*

'I have good memories of Hunter Crescent. I remember as kids sliding down the hill at Morris Young's on oven trays but I do remember a boy sliding down the hill on a carrier bag and doing himself a mischief and ending up in hospital. The downside was the way we were treated by council. We waited months, sometimes years, for repairs. The walls were black with damp and ice on the inside but the council insisted it was condensation. They had lost interest in the housing scheme and the people.'   — *Susan Cushnie Mohammed*

'I stayed at 41 Hunter Crescent with my family, with my dad "Eck" and my mum known as "Wee Peggy". Happy happy memories of my time in the Crescent – we were out all day only going "hame" for your tea. Stayed there for many years and only have great memories of Hunter Crescent – still have many friends I keep in touch with from back in the day.' — *Micheal Morison*

'I was born in November 1957 at No 28C Hunter Crescent. Also, my wee brother Eddie, sisters Donna and Susan – we all attended Goodlyburn. I would just like to thank the world of Facebook that enables old boys like us to keep in touch through the years and more importantly not to forget our route in Hunter Crescent. A special mention to our Granny Glover, who if not for her, we would almost certainly have been put into care. So many happy times in the Crescent.' — *Jimmy Nimmo*

'I lived in Ruthven Avenue from when I was born in 1956 till I was nine years old. I remember a little old lady called Mrs Shaw who used to take a wee group of children on a Sunday to the Church of Nazarene Sunday school. She walked us all down the Feus Road and back. My dad worked for Cappy as a coalman. He delivered in the area and knew everyone. All my family either lived in Ruthven Avenue or Hunter Crescent. So many happy memories and good times.' — *Helen Osborne*

'Hunter Crescent had a great community spirit. Neighbours would feed kids if their mum was out – always looked out for each other. The Tin Hut disco was the highlight of my week; girls on one side, boys on the other, and old Mr Sinclair on the door. Friends that have lasted a lifetime. I learned a lot of life skills in Hunter Crescent. So many memories to tell my grandchildren. God when did I become so old? You can take the girl out of Hunters but never Hunters out of the girl!'
— *Arlene Reaney*

'We lived in the Crescent till 1976. It had a great community spirit, you knew all your neighbours; they would fight but that would usually be the end of it. Seemed we played outside all day, always had something to amuse ourselves from playing "doublers" in the close to collecting "scraps" and swapping them with your pals – kept us occupied for hours. So many great memories of 14C Hunter Crescent.'

— *Lorna Robson (née Shaw)*

'Best years of my life playing outside with my friends, Wendy Ghekis, Jason Furlong, and Maxine Stevenson. Great memories of all my family including my granny and grandad. We used to play for hours at the park and over at the white building after it had been demolished.'

— *Tracy Simpson (née Tanyous)*

'I grew up in Ruthven Avenue between 1968 and 1987. Always seem to spend most of my time up the park called "The Dump", although on one occasion I was shot in the ankle by someone with an air rifle!My parents were quite strict and didn't like me playing out in the streets, so when I seen my dad's car turning into the far end of Hunter Crescent, I would sprint like Linford Christie back into the house! Just like all the other kids, I learned the value of money by earning it at the berries and tatties. Many happy memories in difficult times.' — *Iain Smart*

'I moved to Hunters when I was eleven. It was like moving to a foreign country. I was born in the Meal Vennel, then lived in Forgandenny until age six. We also lived in the Shore Road with the Tay across the street and the South Inch as my back green. We had heard of Hunters, none of it good, and when we moved there it was like moving to a war zone. My granny was raising me while my dad was at the Uni (Perth Penny). Dad was also a graduate of the Universities of Barlinnie and Peterhead. Hunters then, was the last place I wanted to be, however, I settled in, made some friends, and was fine. Looking back from the perspective of many years and many, many miles, Hunters was a tapestry that recorded the wide range of humanity that comprises the Perth working class. We had snobs, drunks, honest working people, and those aspiring to move up the social ladder. That is probably true of every housing scheme. What Hunters has given me is a great affection for working people and a deep resentment of officialdom, the privileged, and, particularly, those people who did nothing to earn their wealth but could stop folks from catching a fish to feed their families.'

— *Harry Smith*

'We first lived in Ruthven Avenue then moved to 19A Hunter Crescent and stayed there till 1987. What I remember was the freedom we had as kids; even playing out in the dark you always felt safe – it didn't feel like the rundown estate everyone spoke about. There was always someone to play with and hang out with. What I don't miss is the stigma and ridicule from outsiders, especially teachers.'

— *Kim Smith*

'I lived at 25F Hunter Crescent with my Aunty Maureen and her girls. Before that, I lived at 19C Ruthven Avenue. Used to play outside for hours, playing games like British Bulldog and Kick the Can. I've got the best memories of my life from that place.'

— *Ray Stevenson*

'All good times. Me, my mum, granny, grandad and aunty all stayed together – we stayed at 20 Hunter Crescent and our neighbours were the Wards, Jerry Riley, and the Stevensons – good neighbours. The streets could be a bit wild at times with punch-ups one day and all forgotten the next. Eventually we got a move to Gowans Terrace – think I almost cried at the news we were moving!'

— *Mary Welsh (née Townsley)*

'Great times and memories. I always remember the close community and the new year's parties – you could walk in and out of each other's houses, towards the end you couldn't do that.'

— *Shuggie Williamson*

'I lived in Ruthven Avenue from 1966 to 1988 – my memory is a bit hazy but had some great times. I can remember in the summer families would be outside playing rounders. We got a hard time from outsiders calling us all sorts – it could be rough but there were a lot of decent people who would look out for each other.'

— *Craig Young*

CHAPTER TEN

Songs and Poetry

Billy Bunters — Berry Bus Song

They say Billy Bunters
The food is mighty fine
A chip fell off the table
And killed a pal of mine
They say in Billy Bunters
The fags are mighty fine
Yee ask for ten regal
They gee yee five woodbine

Memories — Poem

They slagged ye off they put ye doon,
said we came from the poor part o' toon.
He'll steal, he'll lie, that's what they'd say,
some folk widnae gie ye the time o' day.
Aye we were poor to some that's a fact,
but we had riches better than that.
Like singers and dancers, best in toon,
bands like the Mergers beltin oot tunes.
Wi some of our bairns uni they went,
on beer and wine all our money wisnae spent.
We looked after oor bairns some now well kent,
like their folks before them who walked through the toon.
But noo the posh folk cannae put them doon,
because coming fae Hunters was always a test
ye promised yersel to be the best.
And no a loser like folk thought ye'd be,
a drunk a wino like was expected oh ye.
Folk came fae Hunters who are now millionaires,
whove travelled through life and don't have no cares.
There's folk who still live there and will till they die
and some of these folks are better than you and I.
Some of these folks may even be friends of yours,
like the Clayes, the Kellys, the Townsleys or Stewarts.
Or even the Burns, the Cruikshanks and the Broons,
just some of the folk fae the poor part of toon.
So before you go judging on where folk are fae,
here are some words to you I will say.
Never judge people who have less than you,
because even poor people are honest and true.

— **Norrie McLeod**

Wee Hoose in Hunters — Berry Bus Song

I wanna go home
I wanna go home
To my wee hoose in Hunters
And when you get there
They chop off your hair
In my wee hoose in Hunters
The porridge is great
Yee don't need a plate
Yee just need a hammer and chisel
I wanna go home
I wanna go home
To my wee hoose in Hunters

Alice Mcguire — Berry Bus Song

Alice Mcguire peed in the fire
The fire was too hot
She peed in a pot
The pot was too wide
She peed in the Clyde

Auntie Maggie — Berry Bus Song

I went to my auntie Maggie
But my auntie Maggie wisnae in
So I looked through the kitchen windee
She was playing with a corned beef tin

Thank You Billy Bunters

SO HERE I AM at the end of the book. About 33,000 words for five years of writing doesn't seem a lot but I would hate to try and add up the amount of times I started, then within a few days had a wee hissy fit and threw the lot in a drawer, only to be stopped the next day by an old pal from Hunters who would ask:

'*When's the book coming out?*'

or

'*What's happening to the book?*'.

The comments that got me sharpening my pencils were those of know-it-alls:

'*You'll never do it, no way*'.

And as we all know in Hunters:

'*A kneggow eggit eggall kneggows fegguck eggall!*'.

It's only over the last six months that I got my head down and got everything down in some kind of order. I am so glad I did. I have caught up with some old friends and made new ones. I have spoken to people from as far afield as Canada and Australia and as close as Fairfield. Friends and family would jog my memory or I would pester them for names of people who did this or that. It was also very informative getting people's perspective from outwith the scheme. One lady who was a youth worker in the scheme told me that the day she walked into Hunter Crescent, she couldn't help but notice everything was grey – the sky, the streets, and the buildings. Her first encounter with a native of the Crescent was a small boy playing with a box of matches sitting in the street looking up at her:

'*Who are you? ... No another f'g Quaker?*'

he said.

Being sent there after a government study called *Born to Fail* didn't fill her with confidence but forty odd years on, she spoke with great fondness of the people of Hunter Crescent. Despite Hunter Crescent being a housing scheme with a notorious reputation and a hard place to raise a family – an especially difficult place for children who rarely left the scheme even to go to the North Inch – she remembers great kindness, camaraderie, and a community spirit among the residents who were in the main dirt poor but nonetheless tried to help each other when they could.

Another person, an old postie, called Hunters the *Rainbow Scheme*, because of all the *colourful* surnames and large families such as the Browns, Blacks, Whites, Greys, Blues, and Oranges – to name a few. He also recalled running the gauntlet on *Giro Day* with irate residents looking for their money and in between being chased by the infamous packs of wild dogs. Another memory involved two men who *accidentally* found their way into the back of his Royal Mail van: rather than ask the two gents to get out the van, he closed the back doors and drove down to the police station where two local policemen were more than happy to help the two gents out the van... and charge them with breaking and entering.

Now that it is done and I've sat back and let the small brain that I have take it all in, I realise I was one lucky boy in the era that I grew up in. Societal pressure nowadays to have the latest gadgets and wear the current fashions is problematic for youngsters but growing up in *Billy Bunters* it was all about make-do and mend. I can remember playing football in the park with a tennis ball as we had no money to replace the real football we had that died while being garrotted on railway fencing.

As I said in one of the early chapters, none of us had fancy footwear. I can recall one lad playing with wellies on! As for me, I used to wear a pair of brown corduroy boots and loved playing football in them, they were so comfy. Maybe I was too young to care about fashion but never once did any of our gang slate another for what we they were wearing – well maybe Fergie wearing wellies in July. Most of our mums sourced our clothing from the popular jumble sales that used to be held in the City Hall on Saturday mornings.

How great was Hunter Crescent in the 1930s through to the

early 1960s? I don't know, I wasn't there but most of the people that have sent me memories all say it was a great place to live. Only three people got back to me and said they hated it and couldn't wait to get out ... one even said that her happiest memory was the removal van driving out of the scheme. Some people told me that in the 1950s Hunters was already known as a bit of a rough area; and from that time onwards you were housed in there if there were no other houses available. How true that is, I don't know.

The Travellers seem to get the blame for a lot of the ills of Hunter Crescent and people reading this may think I haven't mentioned much about the Travellers. In fact it wasn't until I moved out that I became friends with many.

I am embarrassed to say that when I was younger, if anyone asked me where I lived, I would say Hunters... but the *Good End*. In reality there was no *Good End*. There was good and bad all over Hunter Crescent. When you examine old photographs of the estate it is clear it was one desolate grim-looking place that needed fixing – something the council did not have the stomach to do. The photographs, however, only display the shell of Hunters – the heart was within the houses themselves. I have been inside a lot of homes in Hunters and people did their best to maintain clean, tidy, happy homes.

I cannot help get all dewy-eyed when hearing of the lives of people who have helped fashion my memories and were part of my life, especially those now living in a retirement home, or who are today grandparents and in some cases great-grandparents. The other side of that coin is the sadness I feel for my contemporaries who didn't get out alive due to personal circumstances and lifestyle choices, whether it be drugs or alcohol. Smarter people will say what happened to them was a result of the life circumstances they were born into. It is not for me to judge but I know that many people, good people, have lost loved ones for one reason or another and maybe on some of those occasions the *System* let them down.

When I look back it may have been the beginning of the end of the time when *Children could be Children*. Parents looked after their kids but they also in many ways had a *Tough Love* outlook where it was okay to fall out of a tree, trip up and cut your knee, or pick brambles, eat them, and have gut rot for the rest of the day – without looking for someone to blame. If you got into a fight and ran up the stairs greetin', you would be told to get back out and *'hit them back'* – today the world has gone health and safety crazy.

Maybe we are all guilty of wearing rose-tinted glasses when reflecting on the past. We tend to push the negatives to the back of our minds, such as being stigmatised at school by teachers who had already decided you were probably not going to amount to much or being forced when applying for jobs to use a relative's address, knowing that if you had Hunter Crescent on your *curriculum vitae*, there was a good chance your application form would head straight for the bin.

I have no regrets and made many friends for life. I am proud of where I grew up and have a lifetime of memories, some good and some bad. I have seen great acts of kindness: neighbours helping neighbours whether babysitting, loaning £10 till Friday, or seeing them okay for milk, sugar, or teabags. At the other end of the spectrum I have seen some terrible situations: friends having their electricity cut off and depending on candles for light; evictions where the council simply threw people's belongings out into the street. Thankfully these acts are mostly a thing of the the past.

Not everyone got on. There were big families and the Crescent's big characters – grudges would be held for years and someone who was due a *Bang in the Puss* knew somewhere down-the-line it would be served.

We were living in a bubble as children in Hunter Crescent. We didn't realise we were poor but we were, for the most part, a happy well-rounded bunch of kids. I'm sure other Perth housing-scheme kids, those of Muirton (one class up from Hunters), and those from certain parts of Letham, will find similarities in their lives but Hunter Crescent Crescent 123 has a place in Perth folklore – generations of Perthites will have a story about the place or know someone who lived there.

Well, I did live there and I want to thank all the people I met in my sixteen-year journey in *Billy Bunters*.

Anthony Camilleri, August 2017

ABOUT THE AUTHOR

Anthony Camilleri is very proud of his connection to Hunter Crescent and the local history of Perth. He also has a very keen interest in early cinema and Vaudeville acts naming Laurel and Hardy and the Marx Brothers as his comedy heroes.

Most Sunday afternoons Anthony can be found wandering round a stately home, castle, or palace with his girlfriend Gillian, both of whom are members of the National Trust. Every other Saturday he can be seen pulling out his hair at McDiarmid Park watching his beloved St Johnstone.

Travel is also something Anthony enjoys, with Malta, Italy, and France being three of his favourite destinations.

Being a fan of classic cars he has promised to buy himself a 1938 Talbot-Lago T150-C SS Teardrop Coupé (selling for about £3,500,000) with the sale of this book.

THE PUBLISHER

Tippermuir Books Ltd (*est.* 2009) is an independent publishing company based in Perth, Scotland.

OTHER TITLES FROM TIPPERMUIR BOOKS

Spanish Thermopylae *(Paul S. Philippou, 2009)*

Battleground Perthshire
(Paul S. Philippou and Robert A. Hands, 2009)

Perth: Street by Street
(Paul S. Philippou and Roben Antoniewicz, 2012)

Born in Perthshire
(Paul S. Philippou and Robert A. Hands, 2012)

In Spain with Orwell *(Christopher Hall, 2013)*

Trust *(Ajay Close, 2014)*

Perth: As Others Saw Us *(Donald Paton, 2014)*

Love All *(Dorothy L. Sayers, 2015)*

A Chocolate Soldier *(David W. Millar, 2016)*

The Early Photographers of Perthshire
(Roben Antoniewicz and Paul S. Philippou, 2016)

Taking Detective Novels Seriously:
The Collected Crime Reviews of Dorothy L. Sayers
(Dorothy L. Sayers and Martin Edwards, 2017)

Walking with Ghosts *(Alan J. Laing, 2017)*

No Fair City: Dark Tales From Perth's Past
(Gary Knight, 2017)

The Tale o the Wee Mowdie
that wantit tae ken wha keeched on his heid
*(Werner Holzwarth and Wolf Erlbruch,
translated by Matthew Mackie, 2017)*

FORTHCOMING

The Fair Maid of Perth: the Perth Edition
(Walter Scott, 2018)

All titles are available from
bookshops and online booksellers.

They can also be purchased directly at
www.tippermuirbooks.co.uk

Tippermuir Books Ltd can be contacted at
mail@tippermuirbooks.co.uk

TIPPERMUIR
· BOOKS LIMITED ·